MW00343463

BETTER
PRESENTATIONS

BETTER PRESENTATIONS

A Guide for Scholars, Researchers, and Wonks

Jonathan Schwabish

COLUMBIA UNIVERSITY PRESS ▸ NEW YORK

Columbia University Press
Publishers Since 1893
New York   Chichester, West Sussex
cup.columbia.edu

Copyright © 2017 Columbia University Press
All rights reserved

Library of Congress Cataloging-in-Publication Data
Names: Schwabish, Jonathan A., author.
Title: Better presentations : a guide for scholars, researchers, and wonks /
    Jonathan Schwabish.
Description: New York City : Columbia University Press, 2017. | Includes
    bibliographical references.
Identifiers: LCCN 2016008168| ISBN 9780231175203 (cloth : alk. paper) |
    ISBN 9780231175210 (pbk. : alk. paper) | ISBN 9780231542791 (ebook)
Subjects: LCSH: Business presentations.
Classification: LCC HF5718.22 .S349 2016 | DDC 658.4/52—dc23
LC record available at https://lccn.loc.gov/2016008168

Columbia University Press books are printed on permanent
and durable acid-free paper.
Printed in the United States of America

Cover design: Noah Arlow

For Lauren, Ellie, and Jack,
my sources of infinite inspiration and happiness.

CONTENTS

PART TWO: BUILDING YOUR PRESENTATION

PART THREE: GIVING YOUR PRESENTATION

ACKNOWLEDGMENTS

A book on presentations can only be written if you've given lots of presentations, even bad presentations. And the book can only get better if you've seen lots of presentations, especially good presentations. So I'm thankful for all the people who have watched me present and those who have allowed me to watch them present. I'm especially grateful to those who have provided their feedback and support on my presentations and writing.

First, I thank my publisher at Columbia University Press. This book would not have come together if not for my editor, Bridget Flannery-McCoy, who with patience, focus, and thoughtfulness, taught me how to write for my audience.

Special thanks are due to Robert Haveman and Tim Smeeding, who have been trusted advisors and mentors throughout my entire career.

I'm indebted to the many people who have supported my research and interest in research communication: Greg Acs, Molly Dahl, Doug Elmendorf, Joyce Manchester, Charles Pineles-Mark, John Sabelhaus, Michael Simpson, Tim Smeeding, Julie Topoleski, and others at the Congressional Budget Office, Urban Institute, and other firms and clients with whom I have worked.

I am also thankful to friends in the data visualization and presentation fields who have provided useful feedback, advice, and expertise: Alberto Cairo, Isaac Castillo, Stephanie Evergreen, Steven Franconeri, Tony Fujs, Nolan Haims, Cole Nussbaumer Knaflic, Robert Kosara, Tim Meko, David Paradi, Severino Ribecca, Robert Simmon, Echo Swinford, and Julie Terberg. I'm also grateful to the readers of my blog, PolicyViz, and the various followers and friends on social media and other platforms, whom I all hope to meet in real life one day.

Finally, I could not have maintained the energy and focus this book required without the support of friends and family. My kids, Ellie and Jack, have been sources of inspiration and happiness.

And my deepest thanks to my wife, Lauren, who has edited more than her fair share of chapters, blog posts, and articles. Her love, support, guidance, and intelligence made this book possible.

BETTER PRESENTATIONS

INTRODUCTION

W hether you're a university professor, a researcher at a think tank, a graduate student, or an analyst at a private firm, chances are you follow three general steps when you approach new projects:

PHASE 1. You have a question. You read the literature and collect and analyze some data. Then you spend days, weeks, or months drafting a brief, a journal article, a background or white paper, or a book. You solicit feedback from colleagues and gauge interest from publishers. You revise, revise, revise, and then you submit your document. It's accepted, and finally published.

PHASE 2. As people read the published work, invitations start coming in to speak at various agencies, schools, organizations, and conferences. You start to prepare your presentation by creating slides. You turn some text from your paper into a few bullet points. You copy Figure 1 and paste it in. Add Figure 2 and Tables 1, 2, and 3. Add some more bullet points. Add a slide titled "Previous Literature" with your entire reference list. Add a "Questions?" or "Thank You!" slide at the end. You're done! It only took you a couple of hours and you're ready to take it on the road.

PHASE 3. You stand in front of an audience of 10, 50, 300, or maybe 5,000 people. Many have not read your paper and some may be unfamiliar with the topic. This is your opportunity to convince them of your hypothesis, data, and message. It is an occasion for fostering future relationships, research collaborations, or even funding sources. It may even be a chance for you to convince decision makers or policymakers to implement your ideas. Yet you have only spent a short amount of time thinking about how to effectively present your conclusions, and how to convince your audience that your research, methods, or proposal are worth adopting.

This book is about rethinking Phases 2 and 3 of this process. The work doesn't stop once your paper is published. Giving a presentation is your opportunity to "sell" your results. By "sell" I mean, bring people to your side. Get them to agree with your conclusions, convince them of your methodology or data, and teach them something they can use in their own work or act upon in their own jobs and lives.

When your reader sits down with your paper, she has access to the notes, footnotes, and other relevant details. She can decipher the labels on your charts, and even perhaps work through your equations. When you give a presentation, however, your audience does not have the same opportunity. They are restrained by your pace and choice of content. If your slides are filled with text and bullet points, equations, and complex detailed graphs, your audience might strain to follow you and have difficulty understanding your message. In this case, you are not designing the presentation for your audience; you are designing the presentation for yourself.

Keep this mantra in mind: *Presenting is a fundamentally different form of communication than writing.* Treating your presentation and your paper identically—moving text into bullets, and copying and pasting tables and figures from the paper to the slides—misses this important distinction, and sets your audience up for "death by PowerPoint." It's clear this approach doesn't work: In his annual online survey, author David Paradi consistently finds that the top three things hated by audiences are when (1) the speaker reads the slides, (2) the slides contain full sentences, and (3) the text is too small. We can all relate to the experience of half-listening to a speaker drone on with slides full of text, recounting each bullet point in detail. Yet many researchers, analysts, scientists, and scholars do this in every presentation. Even if you don't have aspirations of a world speaking tour, giving better presentations will help your colleagues, partners, and funders better understand and, hopefully, act upon your work.

You're busy. I get it. Your focus is on conducting great analysis, not on making it "look pretty." You don't have time to create a custom color palette, scour the Web for the perfect image, or learn a whole new set of design skills. This book is not meant to turn you into a graphic designer. However, if you can learn to recognize good, smart design (and utilize things you like and things you don't like), then you can become familiar with some basic aspects of great design such as color, font, and layout, and use these approaches in your presentations. What this book is meant to do is show you *why* you should create more effective slides, and *how* to do so in easier and faster ways.

Many researchers balk at the idea of creating better presentations. "My slides are not there to be beautiful," they say, "they are there so that I can share my research and get feedback on my data and methods." In some fields, dense cluttered presentations are commonplace, and those new to the field stick to this look just to fit in. Little to no thought is given to more effective communication, but long-standing practices are not always the right way forward. Clarity should be paramount. For example, one of the reasons many researchers love the typesetting program LaTeX is because it allows them to present equations, symbols and other complex characters in an open, readable, and clean layout. We should all bring this same precision to our presentations. If your slides are cluttered and disorganized, your audience—even if it's all experts in your field—will have difficulty focusing on what you are trying to say. Giving better presentations and creating better slides is not about "making things pretty," but about recognizing how to communicate and how conscious—and oftentimes simple—design choices can help you do so. I believe researchers can vastly improve the way they communicate their work, and this book is a step toward helping them do so.

If you're a researcher, analyst, scholar, policy wonk, or university professor who publishes research and presents your work to an audience, this book is for you. If you collect, process, or analyze data, and present analysis based on your results, then this book is for you. While I hope other types of presenters will also find this book useful, researchers have unique presentation challenges, especially when it comes to communicating highly technical findings and effectively presenting complex data. The strategies presented in this book address these concerns.

In the shift toward an audience-centric presentation, there are three driving principles:

First, *visualize* your content. The way our eyes and brains work together allows us to better grasp and retain information through pictures rather than just through words (this is known as the "Picture Superiority Effect"). Countless research has tested how people recall words, categories, and text, and how quickly and accurately they do so. Though the actual mechanism by which we are more likely to recall and recognize information when it is presented visually is still a matter of discussion, the superiority of images over text and the spoken word is largely agreed upon. As a presenter, you can harness the power of pictures to create well-designed slides and better data visualizations to help your audience remember and understand more of what you say.

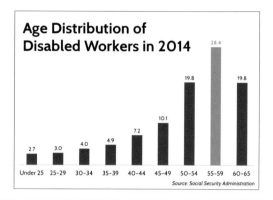

Visualize your content

Second, *unify* the elements of your presentation. This means consistency in your use of colors and fonts, in the formatting of your slides, and in integrating what you say with what you show on the screen. Slide design is not about "dumbing down" your presentation or sacrificing content in the name of making things "pop"; it's about using color, images, and layout to help structure information that help the audience better understand your work. If you toss in a random slide with different colors, different fonts, and a different tone or feel, it can disrupt the flow of the presentation, which disrupts the flow of information and your audience's ability to absorb your content. The consistency of what you say and how you speak—your tone, emotion, and enthusiasm—will help your audience engage with you and

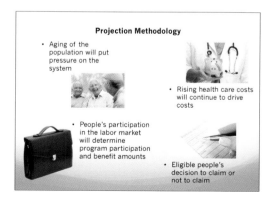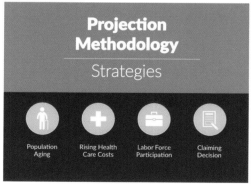

Unify objects on your slides and throughout your presentation

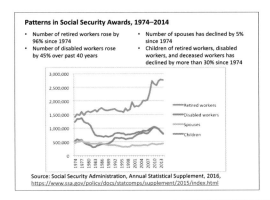

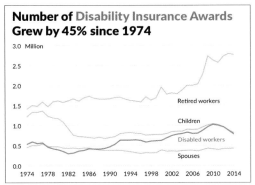

Focus your audience's attention where you want it

more easily understand your message. Your presentation slides are there to support you, not supplant you. This integration is especially important when you show detailed graphs or equations with different terms and labels. You want to verbally guide your audience through these visual elements, and not require them to read details from a distance.

Finally, *focus* your audience's attention on your specific argument. This principle is perhaps the most important. Instead of putting up as much information as possible on every slide (which many presenters do because it's easy and it reminds them to cover each point), keep your slides simple and free of clutter so that you can direct your audience's attention to where you want it at all times. Our attention can often drift and fade during a presentation, and technology has made it easier than ever to become distracted. We can access our email with a simple swipe of the finger and a glance at our phones. Many of the techniques I discuss in this book are aimed at keeping your audience with you by focusing their attention on a specific point, be it text, data, image or spoken information.

These three principles all aim to facilitate the audience's quick and easy acquisition of information. By designing high-quality slides and pairing your spoken word with those visuals, your audience can focus on what's really important—your content and your message—rather than using their energy and attention trying to decipher what's on the screen and how it relates to what you are trying to say.

For the most part, I've kept the "how-to" parts of this book generalizable to any presentation software, but in the instances where I give more specific demonstrations I mainly refer to the Windows version of PowerPoint 2013. Other versions of PowerPoint and other presentation tools such as Keynote, Beamer, and Prezi may include different menus, options, and technologies. However, for most users, the core options around slide design and delivering presentations are fundamentally the same across software tools and platforms. With any tool, regardless of the operating system or when it was released, you can still apply the same kinds of strategies. You will still need to do the nitty-gritty work of visualizing your data, arranging and aligning your text boxes and images, and implementing a uniform color palette. Ultimately, it's not the tool that makes a great presentation, it's the user.

This book does not cover all of the detailed menus available in PowerPoint, nor does it list all the possible online resources available for creating more effective presentations. These options are included in an online companion (*www.policyviz.com/better-presentations*) that contains an updated list of resources, tools, and books related to presentation skills and design. The site also has additional PowerPoint and design tutorials for topics not covered in this book. Sample PowerPoint slides are available to download and modify with your own content.

This book is divided into three main parts to guide your process from presentation conceptualization, to creation, to delivery. Part 1 (chapters 1-3) focuses on planning your presentation. Instead of booting up your computer and immediately inserting text, graphs, and images into your slides, I encourage you to begin by planning, outlining, and writing. The goal is for you to think strategically about your core content and the most effective way to communicate this information to your audience *before* you start creating your slides. These chapters also provide resources and tools for choosing a unified look for your slides, including appropriate and harmonious colors, minimal text, and better fonts.

Part 2 (chapters 4-7) is about building your presentation. I urge you to move away from text- and bullet point-heavy slides and to instead use a mix of text, graphs, and images. These chapters will show you specific examples of better slide design, and demonstrate techniques for focusing your audience's attention where you want it. I also provide strategies for visualizing your data and for unifying what you say with what you show.

Part 3 (chapters 8-9) moves to the practical details of actually giving your presentation. These chapters discuss why practicing can result in better communication, how long your presentation should be, and ways to keep your audience engaged while you speak. I also review technological challenges you might encounter when attaching your computer to the projector. Finally, I talk about creating different versions of your slides for different purposes, such as handouts or posting to the Internet.

The kind of presentation I envision throughout the book is the department seminar, a conference or workshop presentation, an undergraduate or graduate class lecture, or a summary presentation to colleagues, managers, funders, or board members. The proposed approach is particularly relevant for those working with data, which almost always means you will want to show slides (to display tables of statistics or regression coefficients, graphs, and descriptive equations requiring derivation). However, there are times when visuals are unnecessary. Don't feel obligated to use slides if a simple conversation with your audience will suffice. Keep in mind, for example, that very few commencement speakers use PowerPoint. Similarly, you may not need slides for your conference keynote address or a small meeting with four of your colleagues.

If you decide slides are not necessary for your presentation, the very beginning of this book (where I discuss presentation planning) and the end of this book (where I cover public speaking strategies) will be of most use. These sections can help you develop your presentation skills and improve how you deliver your material. Notwithstanding, the majority of the book is dedicated to showing you why strategizing your presentation is important, and how to do it effectively.

PART ONE

DESIGNING YOUR PRESENTATION

THEORY, PLANNING, AND DESIGN

When you begin creating your presentation, try to refrain from immediately opening the computer and starting on a slide deck. The key is to organize first—outlining, writing, sketching, and drawing. This is not to say that you won't revise and edit your slides as you progress. In fact, you may find that building a draft of your slides and then changing, correcting, adding, and subtracting helps you get to a final version. Ultimately, you may decide you don't want to physically write or sketch a draft, but I encourage you to embrace the philosophy of planning your presentation before creating it. Aren't we all taught in elementary school to construct an outline and develop a structure before writing a book report? Why do we pay attention to outlining and planning when we write but prepare presentations on the fly?

HOURGLASS CONSTRUCTION

Planning your presentation before you start creating slides encourages you to think about how the structure of your presentation will differ from the structure of your paper. When you start creating slides, resist the temptation to follow the basic structure of the paper itself, beginning with the introduction, detailing the previous literature, discussing your data and methods, reviewing the results, and then drawing some conclusions. Visually, this construct might resemble a pyramid, starting with the smaller points, then fleshing out the details, and finally ending with the big picture, the bottom-line results and your message.

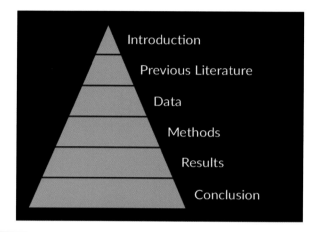

Typical research presentation pyramid

The problem with the pyramid structure is that it doesn't immediately engage the audience. The pyramid structure leaves your audience waiting to see where you are going with your presentation, instead of being able to immediately seize upon the important conclusions and recommendations you are going to present. If you don't share your conclusions or the implications of your work up front, your audience can't see how the various pieces—the previous literature, your data, and your methods—fit together.

News writers long ago recognized some of these issues, and adopted an opposite approach—the inverted pyramid. In this framework, reporters begin their stories with the most relevant pieces of information. The beginning, called the lede, contains the most important parts of the story. From there, information is included in decreasing order of importance. Even if the reader doesn't finish the article, she will likely have covered the conclusions and the most important facts. Also, in the case where a story is longer than expected, the pyramid structure allows editors to cut the end without compromising the focal points of the piece. The reader who gets through the entire article does not finish the last sentence with the takeaway message, but with additional tidbits that back up the crux of the story detailed in the beginning.

While the inverted pyramid brings the important message to the beginning, it doesn't leave the reader with that same message at the end. In a presentation, you should use the opening moments to hook your audience and give them a reason to pay attention. You should then use the closing moments to reiterate that message, placing it utmost in their

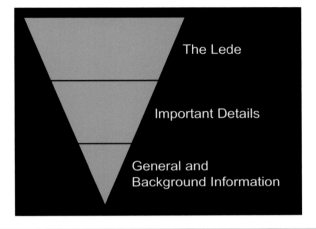

The inverted pyramid in journalism

minds as they leave the room. And use the middle of your presentation for the details and the content (data, methods, and background).

A better structure for a scholarly presentation combines the best of these two pyramids, putting them together to create an hourglass structure. Start with a preview of your conclusions to draw your audience in, and to set your audience's expectations for your entire presentation and argument. Once they know where your argument is ultimately headed, dive

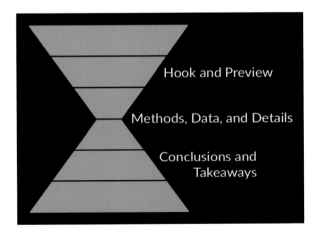

The hourglass structure

into the details and the methodology. But don't end in the middle of the hourglass, buried in the details. Instead, when you conclude, refer back to the broader theme of the importance of your research and what you want your audience to do with your conclusions. Thus, as with a news story, you provide an opening "hook" that immediately engages your audience, but, as in the traditional presentation pyramid, you end by emphasizing your findings and conclusions.

The benefit of the hourglass approach is that you emphasize your conclusions at the points of maximum audience engagement. Your audience is likely to be most attentive at the beginning and end of your talk. At the very beginning, they have just sat down and are full of energy and interest. At the very end, they might ask questions, linger to discuss, or start packing up their things to get to their next appointment. By moving the conclusion to the front, even those audience members who stop paying attention or leave before you finish, will still know your bottom line. Bookending your presentation with your bottom line, and moving the detail and nuance to the middle of the presentation, allows your audience to more readily follow the sequence of your arguments. They are able to see how all the pieces of your presentation fit together, and have a clearer overall picture of your results.

THE PRESENTATION WORKSHEET

When I started transitioning my own presentation philosophy away from the traditional research pyramid structure, I struggled with certain key elements of the presentation. What do I say at the start of my presentation to immediately grab my audience's attention? What message do I want them to walk away with? What comes in between? How do I get my audience to remember my work and my message? To organize my thoughts and structure my presentation, I designed what became a two-page worksheet with key questions to answer prior to building my slides. The worksheet helped me organize my thoughts and condense my message down to a headline. It also helped me carefully consider how my slides could best help my audience understand and remember my message.

In this section, I describe each of the ten sections of the worksheet. The two-page worksheet is available on the book's website (*www.policyviz.com/better-presentations*) for your use.

1. WHAT TYPE OF PRESENTATION ARE YOU GIVING?

- ☐ *Small meeting*
- ☐ *Department or conference seminar*
- ☐ *Classroom lecture*
- ☐ *Sales pitch / funding request*
- ☐ *Keynote address*
- ☐ *Workshop*
- ☐ *Other*

The style, look, and message of your presentation should be tailored to the event and venue. For example, a keynote address in front of a few hundred people may focus on the most important lessons from your work, so you will want large images and very little text. In this case, you won't get into the intricate details of your research, but instead summarize the big picture concepts for your audience.

By comparison, if you are presenting at a small meeting with your colleagues or students, you may want to feature a few, more detailed slides (perhaps supplemented with a handout for closer reading). In such cases, you may want to structure your talk as more of a discussion than a presentation. Accordingly, you may view your role as more of a facilitator than a traditional speaker.

Presentations are about communication and communication occurs between people. Thus, you should start constructing your presentation by thinking about what type of presentation you are going to give, and how your approach will best meet the needs of the people in your audience.

2. WHO IS YOUR AUDIENCE?

- ☐ *Coworkers or colleagues*
- ☐ *Managers*
- ☐ *Scientists/technical professionals*
- ☐ *Salespeople and marketers*
- ☐ *Students*
- ☐ *Mixed*
- ☐ *Other*

This question, like the first, encourages you to think carefully about how your audience will benefit from your presentation, and how your presentation can meet their needs. If you're presenting to a technical audience at a conference, they will want to hear the specific details of your innovative new method. If you're presenting your research in front of a potential funder, the results obtained (and further work you hope to do with those results) might be more important. How will considering who is in your audience change what you will present and how you plan to present it? Instead of focusing too much on the details of the methodology, you may need to ensure there is a bottom-line, actionable message to take away from the meeting.

The language you use might also change for different audiences. You may be better off using less technical language when speaking to the media or a lay audience, but jargon, abbreviations, and technical terminology may be more appropriate for your department lunchtime seminar.

Admittedly, the mixed group is the hardest to prepare for. When speaking to a mix of colleagues, policymakers, students, researchers, and others, try to boil your idea down to its essence. Be clear and be simple. Not dumb, but simple. As Chip and Dan Heath write in *Made to Stick*:

> If we're to succeed, the first step is this: Be simple. Not simple in terms of "dumbing down" or "sound bites." You don't have to speak in monosyllables to be simple. What we mean by "simple" is *finding the core of the idea*. (27)

Finding (and presenting) the core of your idea will work for any audience, but it is perhaps most important for the mixed group. Some portion of your audience will want technical details and some may not. However, all will benefit from hearing a clear, strong, actionable takeaway message. Some research suggests that using words and graphics in your presentations is especially important for people who do not have sophisticated domain expertise (see the "How We Learn" box at the end of this section).

If you're struggling with the right level of detail to include when presenting to a mixed group, identify the specific subgroup you feel is most important to reach—create an audience persona for them, if you will—think about what they need, and target your core message to them.

3. WHAT IS THE HEADLINE MESSAGE OF YOUR PRESENTATION?

For the headline, I only give myself space for one sentence, so that I am forced to boil my presentation down to my core idea. If I want my audience to take away a single message from my presentation, what will it be? In his book, *The Presentation Secrets of Steve Jobs,* author Carmine Gallo refers to these as "Twitter-like" headlines (39): specific, memorable, concise headlines that your audience can easily remember and share. You might imagine your slides as a billboard, showing your message. Your audience should be able to grasp your message easily as you move through your content.

Crafting a concise and active opening statement can be a challenge for many presenters. I usually find researchers in particular have issues with the idea of a headline because they believe their research has details and nuances that can't be summarized in a single sentence or phrase. The goal of a headline is not to trivialize your content or eliminate the complexity, nuance, and subtlety of your research. The goal is to give your audience a single statement that encapsulates your work in such a way that they will remember it, share it, and possibly use it. You can (and will) cover the details during your presentation, but if you can get your audience to remember the headline, then they may come back to you (or your paper) for the details.

If you're having trouble coming up with a headline (or if you think a headline will short-change your work), consider that you probably already have a great model for this kind of conclusion-centric opening—the abstract of your paper. Have you ever read an abstract or executive summary that doesn't tell you *why* you should read the paper and *what* the conclusion is going to tell you? Good abstracts are active, concise, and, importantly, highlight the conclusions of the research. For the reader, the abstract provides an advertisement for the paper. If the abstract does its job well, the reader will be intrigued and want to learn more, finding details about your data and methodology in the body of the paper.

Take your abstract and boil it down to the core. When you present it as your headline message, your audience will know what they are going to learn from your presentation and why it's important to pay attention. For example, "Technology Can Improve Government" can act as a headline and succinctly grab the audience's attention.

4. WHAT DO YOU WANT YOUR AUDIENCE TO DO WITH YOUR CONCLUSIONS?

Consider both your audience and your main goal in giving your presentation. If you are presenting a research paper to your department or agency colleagues, what do you want them to do with your results? Adopt your methodology? Use your data? Give you more data? Understand your findings and assess the reliability of your results? If you are proposing a new program or policy, what should the policymaker, organization, funder, or journalist do with your message? Do you want them to implement your proposed policy, or give you more money to pursue the next part of a wider research agenda?

You don't necessarily need to state this explicitly in your presentation. Sometimes it may go without saying that your goal is to simply share your work and to advance the knowledge in your field, and it would probably be indelicate to announce that the point of your presentation is to attract funding. But even if it's not said aloud, specifically considering your goal and what you want people to do with your message can help you construct a more effective and targeted presentation.

5. CRAFT YOUR OPENING STATEMENT.

You don't have long to grab and keep your audience's attention. Consider your own experience as an audience member: How long does it take before you look down at your phone to check your email or start making a mental list of things you need to do later? The opening of your presentation is crucial for capturing and keeping your audience's attention. This means your opening statement—the first thing you say—needs to be bold and compelling.

Crafting a successful opening statement means avoiding saying something generic like "Thank you for having me", "Maybe you believe this too . . .", or "I am glad to be here." Such openings are boring, have no content, and are repeated constantly. Let's try a simple example. Say you're conducting research on how government is using technology to better respond to citizens' needs. In a traditional opening to this presentation, you might start by saying:

> Thank you for having me. I'm going to talk about some of the work I've been doing on IT needs in the public sector. Before I begin, let me just say that this paper is in progress and I'm still working with the data. I'm also eager to hear any comments or questions you might have, so I'll be sure to leave time at the end.

In this opening, you've told the audience nearly nothing about your work. You begin by thanking the audience, and then basically apologizing for your unfinished work. Your audience is left with no sense of where you are going or why they should listen to you. Instead, try focusing on the takeaway message and the importance of that message:

Changes in technology are enabling governments to respond to citizens in vastly different ways, improving efficiency and reducing costs. Those changes are having real impacts on state governments and specific government programs. I have collected data on 150 state agencies from 25 different states, and will show you how improving internal computer systems leads to a 15 percent increase in citizen satisfaction and a 10 percent decrease in costs. My findings show that states that invest $50 million in their internal computer systems will see positive returns on those investments within 5 years.

In this opening, you immediately engage your audience by talking about why the research is important, what the research has found, and how those findings can be applied to improve governments. The focus is on the conclusions, so the audience knows from the beginning where things are headed.

Use a carefully crafted opening statement as a newspaper article would—with a great hook. Don't be worried that the nuance and detail of your research is not listed in the first 30 seconds of your presentation; you'll have time to dig into those details later. The opening statement puts your headline into words, so ignore subtlety for now and imagine a verbal billboard that will advertise the importance and value of your work.

6. CRAFT YOUR CLOSING STATEMENT.

This is your opportunity to sum up your content and hammer home your takeaway message. In question four, you figured out what you want your audience to do with your conclusions; now it's time to craft a strong closing statement that makes it easy for your audience to embrace your message and act upon it.

In a traditional closing statement, you might end by saying:

My results differ from the existing literature because I've used new, better data, and have modified the theoretic model in a variety of ways. The estimates show that improving internal computer systems lead to a 15 percent increase in citizen satisfaction and a 10 percent decrease in costs, which are both pretty large numbers, right? Thank you for your time and I'm happy to answer any questions you might have.

Alternatively, what if you wrapped your conclusion in a story and demonstrated why your results are important and worthy of your audience's action?

Imagine that you are one of the more than 46 million people who currently receive food stamps. To apply for benefits, you need to take a day off of work—a big deal when you already live below the poverty line—arrange care for your kids, and maybe take a bus or two to the government office. What a difference it would make to be able to submit the application online.

I've shown you how state agencies have improved their computer systems to make these kinds of processes easier and faster. While costing each state about $50 million on average, these changes have raised citizen satisfaction and engagement, and have improved the way they provide services to participants. Either as researchers working in the area of government and technology or in public-support programs like food stamps, or as someone responsible for the computer systems in your agency, I urge you to consider how these technology investments can ultimately improve the lives of people living in your states and your communities.

Here, you've made a direct connection with a person's experience and how the results of your research can help improve that experience. You've positioned the conclusion in a larger framework of the implications of your work, and why your audience should embrace your ideas.

Your closing statement is not necessarily the place to list the details and caveats of your work. You have covered those in the course of your presentation, so there's no need to rehash them (unless, of course, they are particularly important to your conclusion). Focus once more on your headline and highlight the important message you want everyone to take away from your presentation.

While I don't advise you to memorize your entire presentation, I do think memorizing the opening and closing statements can be useful. In general, memorizing your entire presentation raises the possibility of forgetting a "line" and blanking on what you planned to say. Similarly, reading your talk can sound stilted and be boring for your audience (and looking down to read the text breaks your visual relationship with them). However, you do want those opening and closing statements—when you have the most undivided attention—to be polished, concise, and full of content. Take these opportunities seriously and prepare.

7. OUTLINE THE SECTIONS OF YOUR PRESENTATION.

1.   4.
2.   5.
3.

I leave space for five sections here. You may have fewer, but avoid having too many more. Otherwise, it can make it hard for your audience to follow you over the course of your entire presentation. Seminal research by psychologist George A. Miller suggests that we can hold around seven items in our memory at a time; recent research from cognitive scientist Jeffrey Rouder and his colleagues, suggest that we can hold only three or four items in our memory at a time. Maintaining a handful of sections that are clear and obvious will help your audience retain your points.

You might think of these sections as "chapter titles" for your talk. Similar to chapters, they should be oriented around a distinct idea and point. For example, when you talk about the previous literature, what is the main point of that discussion? Do you want to show that you have new data dissimilar from previous researchers? If so, you may want to retitle your previous literature section as "What the research has missed." Maybe you plan on extending previous methodologies in unique and exciting ways—in which case you may consider something like "Advancing the Field." Explicitly writing these section names on a slide for your audience may not be necessary, but defining them for yourself will help you better organize your presentation.

There is another advantage to organizing your presentation into sections: You can reuse sections of one presentation in another. Instead of starting from scratch each time, you can reuse or tweak an existing presentation by inserting or deleting well-defined sections. For instance, a technical section on methodology can be cut when presenting your paper to a less technical audience (e.g., for a keynote), or you may choose to craft your presentation around only your opening and closing sections. If you build your slides in sections, it will be easier to move segments from one presentation to another and to cut and expand when necessary.

Sectioning helps you *begin* outlining your presentation. As you progress and add greater detail, well-constructed slides will begin to emerge. The more you think ahead, plan, and prepare, the more likely you are to build a successful presentation where the audience follows your argument and buys into your ideas.

8. WHAT STORIES CAN YOU TELL?

Another way to relate to and engage your audience is to link your research to relevant stories. By our very nature, we are drawn to the narrative structure of stories, the challenges they present, and the obstacles their characters must overcome. Stories create anticipation and can increase your audience's attention by making it easier for them to relate to you and to remember your content.

Your stories don't need to be funny or emotional or even particularly personal, but they should relate to your content and help advance or support your argument. As a researcher, what stories can you use to connect with your audience? Was there an event that motivated you to undertake this research? Did you talk separately with survey participants or focus groups? Is there a unique data issue that you alone have uncovered? Your stories will stick with people. Your statistics may not.

9. IMAGES (SKETCH OR DESCRIBE BEFORE SEARCHING).

☐ *Graphs & Charts*
☐ *Pictures, Illustrations, & Icons*
☐ *Videos*

From your written report, you may already have the graphs and charts you want to show in your presentation, but you may not need to present every element in detail. Readers often interact with the graphs in your paper in very different ways than your audience will when you project the same graphs on a screen. This means most of the graphs from your paper will need some revision to be effective in your presentation (much more on this in chapter 5). In any case, each graph you use should further your argument; don't feel obligated to include all of the graphs in the paper just because you've already created them. Planning the images you will use in advance encourages you to use only those that are necessary, rather than dumping everything from your paper into your slide deck.

When it comes to pictures, illustrations, icons, and videos, a specific idea of what you're looking for will help you find relevant, useful images—rather than creating generic placeholders. A search for "growth" will give you a 3D column chart with taller and taller columns. Search for "work" and you'll find overeager executives shaking hands cementing their awesome new deal. These stock images are hackneyed and can make your audience see your presentation as tired and unoriginal. Use this section of the worksheet to sketch ideas for images you would like to find, and consider specific keywords you can use to find them. This process will put you, not your search engine, in control of your visuals.

10. ANTICIPATED QUESTIONS AND ANSWERS.

1. *Q:*   2. *Q:*
   A: *A:*

Think about possible questions you may receive and craft your answers. I provide space on the worksheet for you to list two questions you expect to face, but you should obviously be prepared to answer more. I've seen presentations where the questioning has gotten pretty rough—in one instance, the first hand went up before the speaker had even started on the opening slide (economists are not known to hold their punches). Hopefully you won't have to face a tough crowd, but you will be more confident in your material if you prepare.

You may also be aware of some of the shortcomings of your research through conversations with friends, colleagues, or students. Maybe you've already received formal peer reviews, or perhaps there's something you've purposely left out of your presentation because of time constraints that you think people might ask about. Perhaps you're presenting to a specific audience—funders, the media, or policymakers—and can anticipate additional concerns these stakeholders may have, particularly if there's a recent event that brings further prominence to your topic or could heighten the debate. If you take this step seriously, you may identify issues you hadn't considered during the course of your research.

As you prepare your answers, aim to be clear, concise, and to back up your responses with evidence. To get into questions, I like author Alan Hoffler's advice: Instead of asking, "Do you have any questions?"—which calls for a "Yes" or "No" response and may imply that there are no questions—try something like, "What questions do you have?" This makes the audience's questions a welcome part of your presentation and it encourages them to start asking right away. When the Q&A session comes to an end (often better if you lead to it by asking for one final question), take the opportunity to restate your closing statement so that your audience leaves with it in their heads.

FROM OUTLINING TO DESIGNING

Completing the worksheet and expanding sections where necessary will give you the basic roadmap for your presentation. You can then start filling in the gaps and figuring out how to build the narrative of your research over the course of your presentation.

HOW WE LEARN

I derived the core principles of visualize, unify, and focus from watching and delivering hundreds of presentations, as well as studying research in such fields as neuroscience, sociology, and psychology about how we communicate and perceive information. Two sets of theories are particularly useful for presenters who want their audience to better understand and comprehend their message.

The first theory is Cognitive Load Theory (CLT), initially developed by educational psychologist John Sweller in the late 1980s. CLT describes the burden placed on our working memory as we try to hold onto some piece of previous information and then try to process new information. In essence, according to CLT, we can only absorb so much information when it is shared or presented to us.

The second theory is a group of learning principles developed by psychologist Richard Mayer and his many different co-authors (and summarized nicely in his book with Ruth Clark). Mayer's research involves the intersection of cognition, instruction, and technology. Three aspects of his research are especially important for presentations:

1. **The Multimedia Principle** simply states that people learn better from words and pictures than from words alone. Based on a number of studies, Mayer and his colleagues found that there was an 89 percent improvement in learning when pictures were paired with text compared with text alone. (Think: Visualize)
2. **The Contiguity Principle** argues that integrating text and visuals can lead to more learning than when text and visuals are not combined. Over the course of eight different studies, Mayer and his colleagues found that learning outcomes from lessons integrating text and visuals were on average 68 percent higher than those that did not. (Think: Unify)
3. **The Coherence Principle** suggests that adding superfluous elements irrelevant to the teaching goal can disrupt and interfere with learning. Across six different experiments, learning outcomes were 105 percent higher on average for students who received the lesson without extraneous materials than those who did. (Think: Focus)

You have likely witnessed your share of mediocre presentations, where the slides were full of text and bad graphs. You probably tuned out periodically, checked your email, and eventually stopped paying attention altogether. (You may have also seen members of your audience do the same when you were speaking!) Our response to these kinds of presentations can be traced back to how our brains process information as we learn. By recognizing these processes you can improve the way you present your content.

There are a few ways to proceed depending on your preferred workflow. In her book *slide:ology* Nancy Duarte suggests starting your presentation-design process with Post-It Notes, which "allow ideas to be captured, sorted, and re-arranged as needed" (28). I prefer three-by-five-inch index cards because they are easy to move around, transport, stack, and shuffle. On each card, I write down the single message or goal intended for each slide (as with Post-It Notes, their small size encourages me not to cram too much information on each). I then place the stack on my desk (or floor if it's a particularly long talk), which enables me to physically work with the presentation. I often use markers or color pencils to color-code the different sections. It makes it easier to work with the cards before I open the slide software on my computer. I also maintain a composition notebook, where I keep notes, articles, sketch pictures, and draw graphs for presentations I am developing or editing.

Admittedly, this process can be arduous, and you may not have the time or inclination to work in this way. A simple page of notes or document on your computer with your outline or detailed structure of your presentation may work best for you. For some, creating a

Using index cards to help build a presentation (Photo by Lydia Thompson)

rough, working outline in the slide software first and then changing, correcting, and editing the slides works best. I've known some researchers who begin their entire research project by starting in PowerPoint and then writing the paper. I consider my notebooks, index cards, and time spent outlining and sketching an upfront investment for a long-run payoff. My presentation will have my best, most focused attention to detail and organization. I suggest you find a process that works best for you and then refine it over time.

▸ ▸ ▸ ▸ ▸

Now that you've planned what content you want to include, you need to address the look of your presentation. The next two chapters guide you through the basic aesthetic choices for your presentation, namely color and type. The goal is not to try to become a designer but to acknowledge that your aesthetic decisions will affect how your audience views your content. Decisions about which colors to use, how to use them consistently, and where to use them can all affect which bit of text or data series your audience will pay the most attention to. Your decisions about type can establish a hierarchy making it easier not only for your audience to recognize what is most important, but for you to direct their focus where you want it. In designing better-looking slides, we are not aiming for pop or pizazz; we want to add (or subtract) elements that help communicate your content in the best way possible.

THREE THINGS TO REMEMBER ABOUT PLANNING

1. **Visualize.** Organize your thoughts and plan your presentation using a process that works for you.
2. **Unify.** Consider how your presentation will hold together and how it might differ from your written report.
3. **Focus.** Move your conclusion to the front and hook your audience right away. Focus their attention on your content.

PRESENTATION SOFTWARE TOOLS

This book largely focuses on strategies and improvements using the Microsoft PowerPoint software program. However, these strategies—more images, less text, less clutter—should be applied regardless of the software platform used to create your presentations. There are a number of tools currently available to create and manage your presentations. The following is a limited list of possible tools, with more on the book's website.

Beamer. This is a package available with the LaTeX typesetting program. LaTeX is a coding language most often used in technical and scientific documents to set type and mathematical equations. Beamer uses the LaTeX language to prepare slides (or frames, as they are known in Beamer). LaTeX and Beamer are both free programs and work on all major operating systems.

Canva. An online design tool that enables you to create all kinds of design and social media products, including posters, images for social media, infographics, and presentations. Overall, Canva is relatively easy to use, but you may experience difficulties when working with other slide objects such as tables and graphs.

Google Slides. As part of the suite of spreadsheet and word processing tools, Google also hosts a presentation slide platform called Google Slides. It is similar to many other online tools, and can be easily shared between users. You can also download the slides to your computer in a variety of formats including PowerPoint.

Haiku Deck. A mobile-device design platform that enables you to create presentations on the Web and on tablets (primarily the iPad). This tool is essentially a plug-and-play model where you use their pre-packaged images, text, and layout design.

Keynote. Apple's native presentation software is easy to use and works well with video and audio. It has very good zooming and animation capabilities, though, as with PowerPoint's animation tools, they should be used with care. Keynote is available only on Macs, and lacks some of the extra bells and whistles (for better or worse) than PowerPoint.

Prezi. One of the newer online presentation tools, Prezi enables you to create slides in which you can more easily add customized zoom and swipe animations. Unlike some other tools, depending on the version of Prezi you choose to use, you can download your presentation directly to your computer so that you are not dependent on Internet access.

Reveal.js. One of several tools that enable you to create presentations using HTML code. You can grab the code (*http://lab.hakim.se/reveal-js/*) or use the visual editor (*http://slides.com/*). The visual editor includes a free version in which the file size of your slides is limited and your presentations are publicly available. The paid version gives you more space and the ability to keep your files private. One of the advantages of Reveal.js and similar tools is that it is easier to embed online content directly into your slides.

Slide Share and Speaker Deck. These presentation-sharing websites offer the opportunity to post your presentations in their viewing tool, which enables users to view your slides one at a time at their own pace. Depending on the tool you use, you can also easily post your slide notes to the presentation so that users can view them as well.

Zoho Show. Another online toolkit that lets you create, present, collaborate, and broadcast presentations. It also allows some file transfers to and from PowerPoint.

COLOR

We like to think that our work speaks for itself and that the visual appeal of our presentations has no effect on the audience's reception of the content. In reality, the design of your presentation plays a major role in what your audience sees, what they focus on, and how they perceive your message. One study, by New York University Professor Jan L. Plass and others, showed that an attractive visual design (through layout, colors, and imagery) can help evoke positive emotions and foster learning. Employing great design in a technical presentation is not about making your slides "pop" or "look flashy." Instead, employing good design techniques is about unifying the various elements on the screen and focusing your audience's attention on your important points so that they can decide whether or not to buy into your ideas.

The look and feel of your slides will set your audience's expectations, draw them into your presentation, and keep them engaged. These aesthetics are achieved through two primary means: color and type. This chapter will focus on color, and the next chapter will look at type. In this chapter, I discuss how to choose and input a color palette, where to use those colors on your slides (both in the background and in your text or graphs), and how color can make your slides more appealing to your audience.

Maureen Stone, a pioneer in the area of color research and author of the book, *A Field Guide to Digital Color* wrote that, "Color used well can enhance and clarify a presentation. Color used poorly will obscure, muddle, and confuse." Color can be used to organize your slides, to clarify your data, to draw attention and direct the eye, or to set a mood. Reds, for example, evoke passion, excitement, and energy; blues, harmony, peace, and calm; yellows, sunshine, excitement, and energy.

Many presenters simply use black and white, which is easy to implement (it's the default), familiar to our eyes and brains (for example, most printed books), and has very high contrast (black text stands out clearly on a white page or slide). As important as these advantages are, black and white do not tap into the natural appeal of color and, especially for purposes of presenting research and data, the utility of color.

Consider the following two slides. The first slide, using only black-and-white colors gives the audience everything they need without focusing attention on any particular region of the slide. It tells no story and gives the viewer no sense of what to focus on. The second slide simply adds green to the bar on the right. Doing so highlights the last bar and draws the audience's attention to that single data point.

If you're presenting charts and graphs of any complexity, for example, color will direct the audience's focus. You're probably already using color in your graphs anyway, but you can likely do so more strategically. Could your scatterplot with forty different points benefit from adding color to highlight different clusters? Even if you prefer to use the default slide format—black text on a white background—you might add a high-contrast color to emphasize certain words or highlight particular data points or patterns in your graphs. How does your black-and-white column chart differ when you add a single green bar that highlights a specific number or finding? In the data visualization chapter, I explore these tactics in more detail, but for now I'll focus on general strategies for picking and using colors across your presentation. By using the same colors in your graphs, text, and elsewhere in your presentation, you can achieve unity and give your presentation visual coherence.

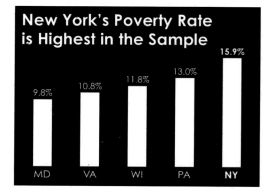 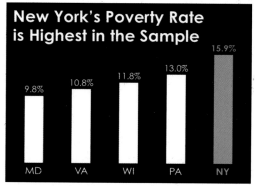

Using color with black and white

CHOOSING A COLOR PALETTE

So, how do you choose and use appropriate colors to help you build highly visual, unified, and focused slides? Picking colors is not easy, even for seasoned graphic designers, so many of us just defer to the default swatches in our software tools. These aren't necessarily *bad* colors—you may like the default color palette in the Microsoft Office package. The prevailing problem is that *everyone* uses those default colors, which means everyone's slides look the same. Choosing a different color palette will help make your presentation stand out.

The first task is to determine how many colors you need in your palette. The Microsoft Office package provides you with four "text/background" colors (the first four colors) and six "accent" colors, each with five tints and shades.

Personally, I usually don't need more than three or four colors in my palette (plus black, white, and gray)—two or three colors for text and for use in graphs, and maybe one more for complex graphs or slide objects that need special highlights. Consider, for example, the color palette for the Urban Institute, a nonprofit research organization in Washington, D.C. where I began work as a researcher, and data visualization and presentation specialist in 2014. The main colors in Urban's palette are cyan, gray, and black; yellow and magenta are used as secondary colors (the full color palette also includes shades of cyan, gray, and yellow, and is publicly available at *http://urbaninstitute.github.io/graphics-styleguide/*). When using this palette in presentation slides, blue, yellow, and white contrast strongly off a black background, and black and white work well on a blue or gray background.

I developed three other sample color palettes using a variety of websites, resources, and images. Notice how each includes light and dark colors that can be easily swapped for background and text colors. Each also includes a "bright" color that could be used for highlighting

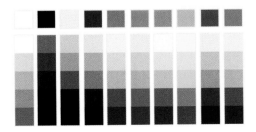

Sample color palette from PowerPoint 2013

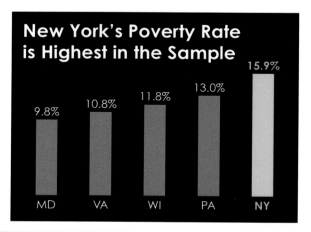

Using color palettes in slide creation: The Urban Institute palette
(Source: Data from U.S. Census Bureau, 2014)

key words or in graphs. White, black, and variations in gray can also be used for many purposes, such as text, outlines, and other shapes. I've only picked four colors for each palette,
though more could be added if needed. (I'll refer to this slide throughout the chapter to demonstrate how color can affect your audience's perception of your slides. The graph was made in
Microsoft Excel and the font is Century Gothic.)

Each of these four palettes use high contrast to accentuate the last column. In the slide
that uses the Urban Institute palette, the blue bars stand out on the black background, and
the yellow bar for New York stands in contrast to the rest of the slide. Similarly, the green
bar in the top slide pops out to the viewer, with the rest of the colors in shades of blue to
provide more subtle contrasts. The other two slides use a lighter background, with the
bottom slide using bright blues and reds and the middle slide using a more muted palette.
All four present the exact same data, but the different backgrounds, text, and graph colors
provide different aesthetics.

Notice that each of these palettes has a set of associated color codes. These codes tell
the computer how to render the color on the screen (and on the printed page). There are a

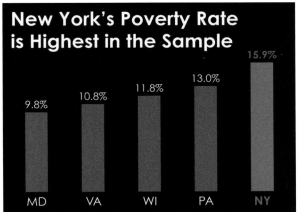

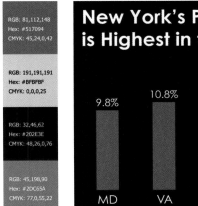

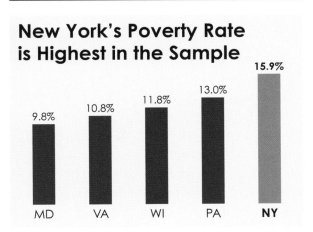

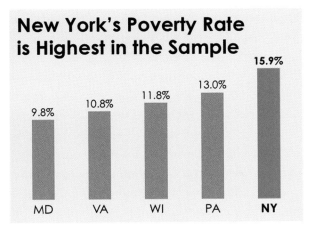

Sample color palettes for slide creation

variety of color models that can be used for different purposes, from web design to print. The codes included for the colors above represent three of the more common color models. They are:

1. **RGB.** These are the colors your computer "sees," and are described as a combination of red, green, and blue light (hence RGB), each value within a range of 0 to 255. When all three values are set to zero, there is a complete absence of color and the screen is simply black; when all three are set to the maximum value, 255, you achieve the highest value, white. All other colors fall somewhere in between.

2. **Hex.** The "hex triplet" color code is a six-digit hexadecimal number used in computer applications. This system corresponds directly to RGB—for every RGB value, there is an associated hex triplet. You can convert between the two using web tools such as "RGB to Hex" at *www.rgbtohex.net*.

3. **CMYK.** The CMYK color model stands for cyan (C), magenta (M), yellow (Y), and black (K). If you open your color printer, you will see four cartridges matching each color type. Unlike the RGB and Hex color models, CMYK is a *subtractive* color space and describes the amount of ink on the printed page. CMYK color codes are represented as percentages: all four values are set to 0 percent for white; for black, the C, M, and Y codes are set to 0 percent and K is set to 100 percent. While there are tools for converting between this model and other color models (such as *www .codecrete.net/CMYK*), not all the colors in one space are necessarily available in other spaces. Browns in particular are difficult to represent on screen and intense blue hues are difficult to reproduce in print.

For most of us, the exact differences between these color models will not affect how we use color in our slides. Their main utility is in translating colors out in the world into our slide software. Say, for instance, you want to use one of the colors in one of the palettes above for some text. In PowerPoint, you can navigate to the color menu from the *Font* or *Format* menu and then choose "More Colors." Once you've inputted the color, you will see it listed under a new section called *Recent Colors*, which you can now use for other slide objects or text. Similarly, if you're using Apple's Keynote program, the *Style* menu in the *Text* tab will allow you to input the color codes. If you're using the LaTeX-based presentation package Beamer, you can simply define your colors directly, according to the RGB code with a command like "\definecolor{SchwabishBlue}{RGB}{22, 150, 210}".

With tools like PowerPoint and Keynote, you can create reusable color palettes for use in other presentations or to share with others. To do so in PowerPoint, you can create a *Theme* (available under the *Design* tab) to add different layouts and fonts to a color palette. One advantage of creating a *Theme* in PowerPoint is that the color generator will fill in the different tints and shades of your primary color, just as in the default palette.

A LITTLE COLOR THEORY

A little color theory can illuminate why these palettes work—and can guide your choice of which color in your palette should be used where and in what combination.

The basic color wheel is simply a circular arrangement of colors showing the relationship between different classes of color. *Hue* is the named description of color, like "red" or "blue." This is typically how we define and identify colors. The color wheel is arranged in such a way that warm colors (reds, yellows, and oranges) sit on one side, and cool colors (blues, greens, and purples) on the other. This categorization—and the relationships

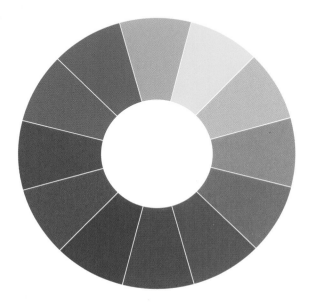

Basic color wheel

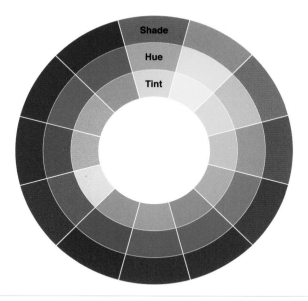

Basic color wheel showing hue, tint and shade

of colors across the color wheel—will help you figure out where and how to use colors. Once you understand the basic relationships, you can modify certain attributes of your colors. By doing so, you can make certain aspects of your slides (such as text, graphs, and shapes) stand out and draw focus.

After hue, the next important color attribute is *value*. The *value* of color (sometimes called *lightness*, *luminance*, or *tone*) is adjusted by adding black or white. Adding white to the color—known as adjusting the *tint*—moves you toward the inside of the color wheel. Similarly, *shades* are darker values that are created by adding black to the hue, and move you to the outside of the color wheel.

As an example, consider this slide with a blue background. As I darken the background by adjusting the *value* of the blue, it may make other parts of the slide easier or harder to read as the contrast (discussed in detail below) changes. In general, when working with colored backgrounds, dark colors usually work better because we perceive cool colors to recede away from us, as described by presentation author and speaker Garr Reynolds in his book *Presentation Zen Design*. By comparison, warm colors seem to advance or appear more active, which is why they often work best as foreground objects such as shapes,

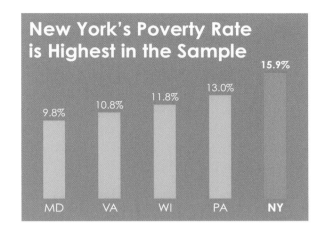

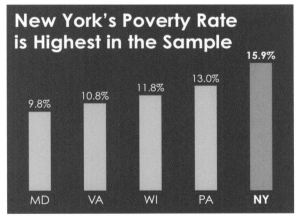

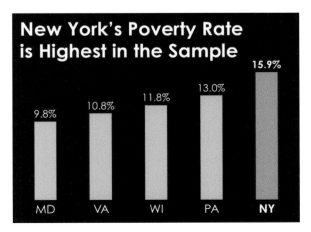

Varying the value

POWERPOINT COLOR TOOLS

Each of the color attributes of hue, value, and saturation can be adjusted using the standard color picker available in most presentation software programs. The image on the left, from PowerPoint 2013 on a Windows computer, allows you to select the hue, adjust the saturation by moving up or down in the colored rectangle, and then change the value by using the slider on the right. Similarly, in PowerPoint 2011 on the Mac, you can select the hue, adjust the saturation by moving the cursor around the circle, and change the value by moving the slider on the right.

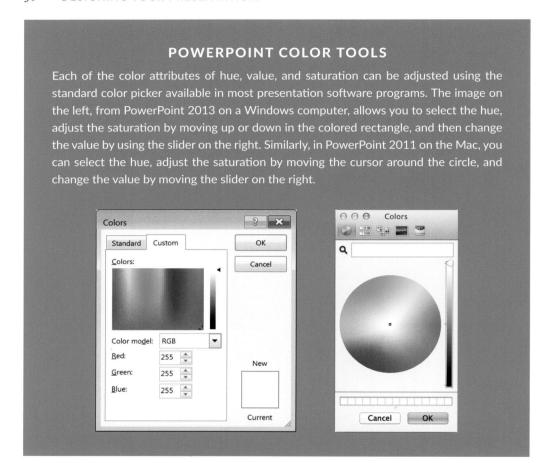

text, or graphs. In this example, the slide with the darkest background has the sharpest contrast, and the warmer colors of the bars and text tend to pop out more and appear to come toward you.

You can also adjust the *saturation* (or *chroma*) of color by adjusting the relative purity of the hue; you might think of adjusting saturation as making the color brighter or duller. Adjusting the *saturation* will move you from rich colors to earth tones and eventually to colorless shades of gray. In this example, I reduced the *saturation* of the background purple color. It doesn't necessarily become darker (I'm not adjusting the *value*), but instead approaches gray. Going the other way along the *saturation* spectrum generates a richer purple.

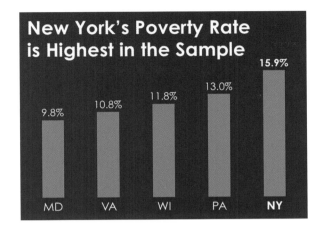

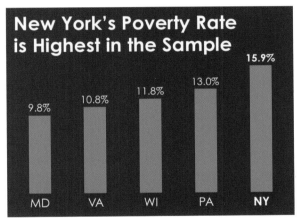

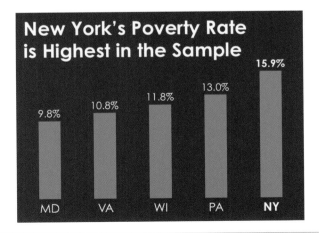

Varying the saturation

As these examples indicate, one of the most prominent colors in your presentation is the slide background. Often, presenters use a white background, but using a light or dark color from your palette will allow you to create slides that look and feel unique and facilitate your use of other colors to draw attention to specific elements on your slides.

Which color background you choose depends on a variety of factors, including the kind of presentation—big keynote, department seminar, or small meeting—and whether you're in a light or dark room. If you are in a well-lit smaller room, you may be better off using a light background, because placing light text on a dark background can sometimes look washed out in such settings. Also, we are accustomed to reading dark text on a light background, so this may feel more natural to an audience, especially in a small room where the audience is seated close to the screen. I've heard some people worry that standing in front of a screen with a light background will show your shadow more than a dark

FORMATTING THE BACKGROUND IN POWERPOINT

To format the background color in PowerPoint, either select *Slide Background* from the *Design* menu or right-click on the slide and select the *Format Background* option. Both will bring you to the standard formatting menu where you can choose colors, gradients, pictures, or patterns. You can use the *Master View* in PowerPoint to format the background color for your entire slide deck at one time. The *Master View* also allows you to place elements that will appear on all of your slides, such as a logo, date, or website. Though I find very little need for these kinds of objects (as I'll discuss further in chapter 4), the *Master View* can be helpful if you need to include repeated objects such as a disclaimer notice or branding for your organization. (Note: If you add an element to the *Master* slide, it cannot be deleted from an individual slide; it's now locked and can only be changed by going back to the *Master View* or inserting a slide from another file that uses a different *Master* template.)

If you paste slides from one presentation file to another in PowerPoint, the slide design in the new presentation will be applied to the slide you are pasting in. When you paste the slide into the new file, a small clipboard icon appears. To maintain the format of the original slide, click the arrow on the right side of this icon and select the *Keep Source Formatting*. (Note: This will bring over the formatting in the Master slide, so you may need to do some additional editing later on.)

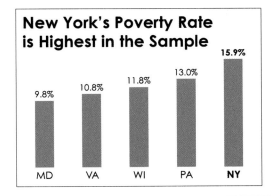 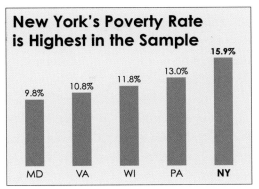

Using gray instead of white in a well-lit room

background. Personally, I don't think this is something to be too concerned with, especially in department seminars or conference presentations.

However, a very light or white background can sometimes feel a bit too bright—even blinding—especially if you are presenting in a small room that is dark or poorly lit. In such cases, one strategy you can use to avoid the blinding white is to use a light gray or light-colored background.

If you are in a dark or a particularly large room (think keynote address), a dark background will often work better. Author Guy Kawasaki, former chief evangelist of Apple,

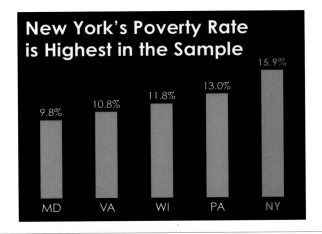

A dark background for a dark room

advocates always using a black background because it is more serious and makes the slides easier to read than a bright white background. While I'm not a staunch follower of this rule, I do find that slide objects tend to stand out more against dark backgrounds in darker rooms.

Most presentation software tools also offer alternatives to a single, solid color for your background as defaults. In PowerPoint, many of these defaults (look under the *Themes* or *Background Styles* menus) include unnecessary and distracting elements such as boxes, crazy shapes, and colors that are too pronounced. In general, I recommend avoiding these busy templates. Even subtle background shapes, textures, and gradients, can often add unnecessary clutter to my slides and distract the audience from my content.

USING COLOR CONTRAST

Whatever background you decide to use, you will need to pair that color with those for other objects you plan to show including text, graphs, and other shapes. One of the most important things to consider when choosing your colors is contrast. Irrespective of the color palette, sufficient color contrast will make it easier for your audience to read your content, and easier for you to direct their attention.

You can use the color wheel to design a color palette with sufficient contrast, or to adjust color combinations within your palette to increase the contrast between elements. There are many strategies you can employ to achieve contrast, but here are four of the most common ones:

1. *Monochromatic colors* sit along a single radius of the color wheel and feature a single hue, but tints and shades vary the value of that color. A monochromatic color palette gives a more unified look to your slides. Such palettes are fairly easy to create because you only need to choose a single color to work with. Implementing a *monochromatic* color palette is especially easy in PowerPoint, because the color palette tool automatically generates different tints and shades of each color. In most programs, you can also adjust the value of a hue by changing its *transparency*, available in the *Format* menu in PowerPoint for example. To get high contrast within the monochromatic palette, try to take colors from either end of the *value* spectrum.

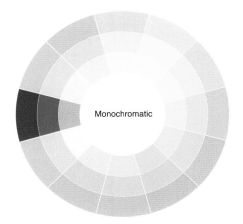

The monochromatic palette

2. *Complementary colors* sit on opposite sides of the color wheel. Using complementary colors in your palette is an easy way to ensure you have colors with significant contrast. When used at full saturation, complementary colors can look especially vibrant, but may also be a little too strong, which you can ameliorate by adjusting the value or saturation of the colors.

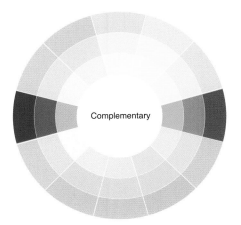

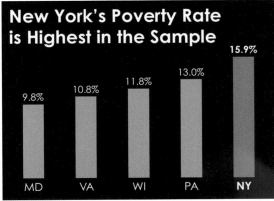

The complementary palette

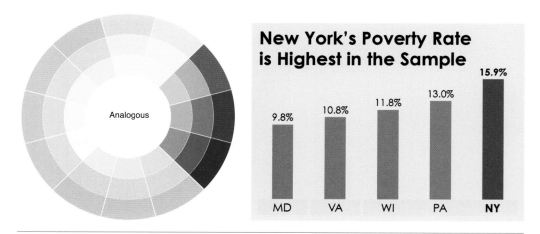

The analogous palette

3. *Analogous colors* sit next to each on the color wheel. Using analogous colors will give your slides a unified look because the colors are so close in hue. Implementing an analogous color palette may be more difficult because you will need to choose the individual colors and then input them into your slide software (unlike a monochromatic color palette, for example, for which slide software will usually generate shades and tints for you automatically).

4. *Achromatic colors* have no hues, only black, white, and shades of gray. For many researchers, this is the true default color palette. An achromatic color palette is ex-

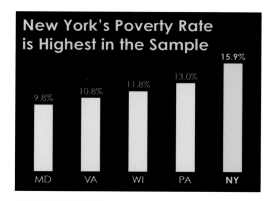

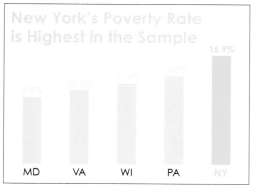

The achromatic palette

tremely easy to implement in a presentation: select some (bright) color to pair with the black and white. If you decide to do a black-and-white presentation, I strongly recommend you choose just a single color when you want to highlight a specific aspect of your slide such as some text, part of a graph, or other object. You'll notice that not all color combinations work, however; for example, yellow text on a black background has high contrast, but it is almost impossible to read that same yellow text on a white background.

According to the NASA Ames Research Center, the "most important aspect of color choice in graphics is luminance [value] contrast." This makes sense—*value* (or luminance) is, loosely speaking, the aspect that dictates the visual brightness between two colors. Thus, sufficient contrast on this dimension should produce the best legibility. In short, our eyes are more sensitive to changes in value than to changes in hue or saturation. This is why black and white are such an effective pair; they have neither hue nor saturation and sit at opposite ends of the value spectrum. Similarly, lighter green text will be more legible on a black background than a darker green because the color's value is being adjusted. (Note: The two greens in the slides below are taken from the default palette in PowerPoint 2013.)

You'll notice that none of the palettes in these examples use combinations of reds and greens of similar intensity. This is because (according to Gegenfurtner and co-authors in *Color Vision: From Genes to Perception*) about nine percent of men and one-half percent

 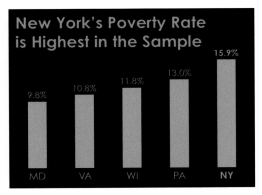

The power of value

of women have some form of color vision deficiency or color blindness. There are different types of color blindness, the most common being difficulty discerning between certain shades of greens and reds (called "deuteranopia"). Not *all* red and green color combinations are challenging; however, it's all about contrast. Red and greens that have high contrast (different values) will be easier for people with color blindness to distinguish between, while low-contrast colors will be harder—perhaps impossible—to distinguish between.

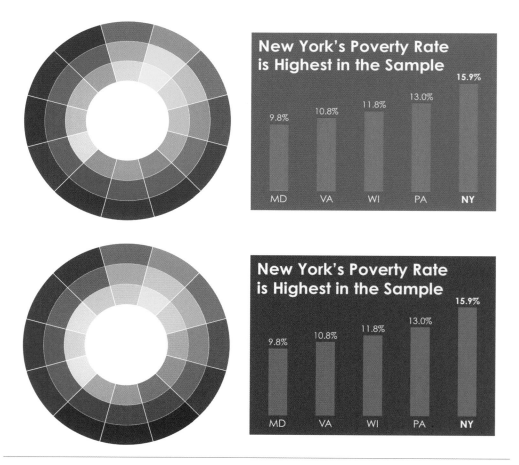

Designing with color blindness in mind

THE RAINBOW COLOR PALETTE

The continuous rainbow color palette can introduce false thresholds in the data because the palette does not map onto our number system. For example, when your data shifts from 3 to 4, you may see very little or no perceptual difference in the shades of green. However, making a similar unit shift from 5 to 6 may move you from light blue to dark blue.

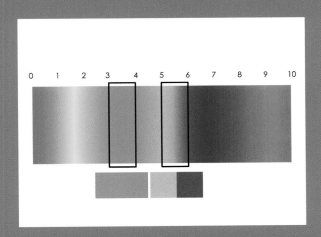

In 1996, IBM researchers Bernice Rogowitz and Lloyd Treinish showed that using the continuous rainbow color palette could hide conclusions gleaned from images whereas visuals using palettes that better map to the human perceptual system showed the results more clearly. In a more recent 2011 study, Michelle Borkin and colleagues redesigned a diagnostic test for heart disease, moving from the traditional 3D representation with a rainbow color palette to a 2D visualization with a diverging color palette. Overall, they found that moving from 3D to 2D reduced diagnostic errors by 21 percentage points, and moving from the 2D-rainbow color palette to the 2D-diverging color palette reduced errors by 29 percentage points.

Bottom line—try to stick with a discrete set of colors to ensure your use of color clarifies, not confuses, your audience.

There are a few (free) tools you can use to check the contrast of your color palettes, both for legibility for those with visual impairments and for generally good use of contrast. In particular, I like Contrast Checker, WebAIM, and David Paradi's Color Contrast Calculator. Each tool scores your selected colors by testing the contrast with the Web Content Accessibility Guidelines (WCAG) developed by the World Wide Web Consortium (W3C). The WCAG covers a range of recommendations for making online content more accessible for people with disabilities, and easier to view for users in general. Also, free tools such as Color Oracle, the Coblis Color Blindness Simulator, and Vischeck enable you to test your images and color palettes to ensure they are appropriate for people with various vision limitations. A more low-tech method, suggested by author Matt Carter, is to print the slide in question on a black-and-white printer or use your computer's printer preview options to view the slide in black and white.

In general, when it comes to color, and especially to contrast, trust your instincts. If you find a slide hard to read on your computer, it is likely your audience will find it even more difficult in a presentation.

CREATING YOUR OWN COLOR PALETTE

Once you start thinking more seriously about the use of color in your presentation, you may want to explore beyond the default color palettes available in your presentation software tool. In this case, the Internet is your limitless reservoir for inspiration, resources, and tools. There are a wide variety of online—often free—color-picking tools that provide examples of color palettes. If you're so inclined, online options can enable you to create your own color palettes. I list a few here with more available on the book's website:

ADOBE COLOR. This is a popular and easy-to-use tool that allows you to play around with colors, either by typing in different color codes (for example, RGB or HEX) or by manually moving sliders around the color wheel. There are preset guides to help you create different color schemes (e.g., monochromatic, complementary, or analogous) by simply choosing one color and then using the selectors to create a full five-color palette. You can also browse the color palette gallery to use palettes others have created.

COLOR BREWER. Originally designed for adding color to maps, Color Brewer allows you to select from predefined color palettes that are consistent across a number of dimensions: number of data classes; type of data (e.g., sequential, diverging, qualitative); single- or

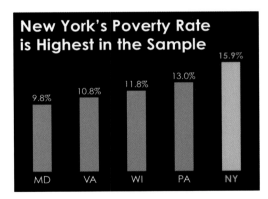

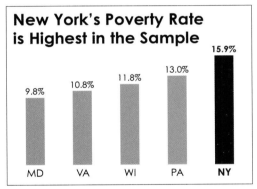

Color palettes created using photos from Unsplash.com
(Photos by (top left) Todd DeSantis and (top right) Hernán Lucio)

multi-hue; and colorblind-, photocopy-, and print-safe. One you've selected your palette, you can record or export the resulting color codes.

COLOUR LOVERS. This site is geared toward the creative community. Instead of providing you with a specific color picker or generator, the site features other people's palettes. It also hosts a great library of other color tools and creators.

DESIGN SEEDS. This website contains a collection of color palettes derived directly from photographs. The color palettes have more of a real-world feel to them because you see exactly where they come from. If you can visually connect your content with an image, you may be better able to use the color palettes provided on this site for your own presentation.

You can also create your own palette from scratch. Because I'm not a graphic designer, I tend to start with colors I see around me or online, or ones created by actual designers. If you like the colors in the University of Wisconsin logo or in the advertisement from the Gap, they can be used as a starting point. If you think the colors in the picture of your kids playing t-ball would work well on a slide, then use those. There are any number of color extraction tools to get those colors from the website or image and into your slides. Most of these programs work in the same way: You get the color codes as you direct your mouse over the color in the image you wish to use. Keynote and modern versions of PowerPoint have this kind of tool built into the program. *DigitalColor Meter* is a native program on the Mac operating system that works in the same way. There are also free third-party programs for use on Windows computers such as *Instant Eyedropper* and *ColorCop*.

Consider the two images on the previous page. I extracted four colors from each, using extreme light and dark colors for use as the text and backgrounds, and then a couple of accent colors to use in a graph or other slide objects to draw and focus attention. The entire process of finding an image, extracting the colors, and testing them in my slides took about 30 minutes.

▶ ▶ ▶ ▶ ▶

Regardless of how you choose your colors, remember that color is a powerful tool in your effort to engage your audience, visualize your content, and focus people's attention.

THREE THINGS TO REMEMBER ABOUT COLOR

1. **Visualize.** Color matters—use it carefully and strategically to highlight important parts of your presentation.
2. **Unify.** Be consistent with your use of colors throughout your presentation.
3. **Focus.** Use color to draw your audience's attention to specific parts of your slides.

TYPE

The principle of focus leads me to urge you to put *less* on your slides—less text, less clutter—all with the goal of helping you guide your audience's attention to what is actually important. Text is another aspect of design that presenters don't always consider, and yet it can make an enormous difference for your audience. When text is used, it should be used with purpose. As with color, the choices you make regarding the look of your text affect what your audience sees and their overall perception of your presentation. The importance of the design of your text is aptly summarized by authors Erik Speikermann and E. M. Ginger: "Anyone looking at a printed message will be influenced, within a split second of making eye contact, by everything on the page: the arrangement of various elements as well as the individual look of each one. In other words, an overall impression is created in our minds before we even read the first word" (39). So before you begin putting text on your slides, take some time to think about how the text will eventually look.

This chapter focuses on using multiple fonts in better ways. However, as emphasized above, putting *less* text on each slide is an important strategy in drawing your audience's focus toward you rather than merely reading the slide. See the next page: the typical text-heavy slide on the left has far too many words, the text is too small, and it uses the black (default) Calibri font on a white background. The revised slide on the right uses the Cabin font (which I think works well in presentations because it has nice spacing between the letters and there is a big difference between the regular font and the bold font) and reduces the number of words (which allows the size to be increased significantly). I've also used color to distinguish the title from the body of the text, and switched to a

Mortality Trends in U.S. Adults

- Since 1999, mortality among middle-aged (45–54) white Americans has increased
- Increase is most likely due to problems with legal and illegal drugs, alcohol, and suicide.
  - Accidental poisonings increased more than all other causes combined
  - Obesity- and smoking-related diseases also contributed to observed patterns
- 2013 mortality rate in U.S. is about 1.25x rate in France
- Long-term improvements in mortality rates largely due to better medical treatment, preventative measures, lifestyle changes, and decline in smoking.
- Increase is especially pronounced among women
- Between 1992–1996 and 2002–2006, female mortality rates increased in 43% of U.S. counties
- Women's health, especially, has profound implications for the health and well-being of children and families

Mortality Increased among Middle-Aged White Americans

Between 1999 and 2013, mortality rate increased by 0.5% per year

Most likely due to drugs, alcohol, and suicide

Increase among women larger than among men

Reducing text and increasing font size
(Source: Aron et al, 2015; Bernstein and Achenbach, 2015; and Case and Deaton, 2015)

gray background to ensure that the background isn't too bright. Further reducing the text or using visuals will focus the audience's attention on the content (an approach discussed in later chapters).

MAKE YOUR TEXT BIGGER

My first piece of advice is simple but crucial for your audience: Make your text bigger.

When inserting text into your slides, design for the person at the back of the room. Your slides should look more like a billboard—large type, simple, direct, and memorable—than like a printed page of your report. Don't be limited by the default sizes of 12 pt, 14 pt, 16 pt, and 18 pt; maximize the text size to fit the available space. You should usually be going to 28 pt, 36 pt, 48 pt, or higher. Some authors recommend a minimum font size of 28 pt; this is a reasonable rule of thumb, but be aware that some fonts can appear smaller than others due to letter thickness or letter spacing. Text is rarely too big, but it is very often too small. For slides with a single headline and few details, I try to use font sizes that are at least 45 points. Not only will increasing your font size help you to design for the back of the room, space limitations will force you to put less text on each slide.

Overview of Social Security	**Overview of Social Security, 2014**
• About 39 million people received retirement benefits in 2014 • Nearly 3 million people received benefits as spouses or children of retired workers in 2014 • About 11 million people received disability benefits in 2014 　– Most disabled beneficiaries between ages 55 and 65	About **39 million** people received retirement benefits Nearly **3 million** people received benefits as spouses or children of retired workers About **11 million** people received disability benefits (most ages 55 to 65)

Text for the back of the room
(Source: Data from Social Security Administration, 2016)

To test whether your type is sufficiently large for your audience, zoom out your slides to 50 or 60 percent (in PowerPoint, you can do this using the slider at the bottom right) or simply walk to the other side of your workspace. If possible, test your slides in the room where you are going to present. If you can't test your slides in the exact room you are going to use, using an actual projector instead of your computer's monitor will help you get a sense of

Make your text bigger

whether the size of your text will work. If you can read the slides easily, then your audience should be able to as well.

UNDERSTANDING AND CHOOSING A TYPEFACE

In addition to size, another major text design decision is the font or typeface (the two terms have different meanings, but are often used interchangeably). Fonts can be categorized into three general groups: serif, sans serif, and script. Serif fonts are those with extending "feet" at the end of each character, while sans serif fonts do not. Script typefaces use curly letterforms and may drop below the baseline on which the serif and sans serif typefaces typically sit.

In the following three slides you can clearly see the difference. The first slide uses the sans serif font Aller. The second uses the serif font Times New Roman, a font most people are probably familiar with from word processing programs. The last slide uses the *Apple Chancery* script font. You can see the differences in the letterforms in the three slides; for example, examine the letter "k" in the word "stroke" and notice how it differs across the three font types.

Sans serif fonts are best for presentations. The letterforms are usually thicker than serif fonts; furthermore, the feet on serif fonts can sometimes get lost in projectors with low resolution levels. In one study by Jo Mackiewicz from the Illinois Institute of Technology, respondents reported that sans serif fonts appeared more professional and were more comfortable to read than serif fonts. In another study, Hyunjin Song and Norbert Schwarz from the University of Michigan found that fonts that were harder to read led respondents to judge a task as harder and less likely to be undertaken. I typically reserve my use of serif fonts for when the text is going to be very large or when my slides are going to be used as a printed document and not shown on a screen.

The font you choose for your slides can shape the tone and feel of your presentation and affect your audience's perception of your content, so spend some time exploring the default font library on your computer or find other fonts to use (I'll show you how later). A true font *family* will consist of a group of fonts with different sizes and weights. For example, the standard Arial font family includes the usual Arial font, but also **Arial Bold** (notice how it differs from the boldfaced version of **Arial**) and Arial Narrow. You can mix different fonts within the same font family to add diversity to your slides, to generate hierarchy between

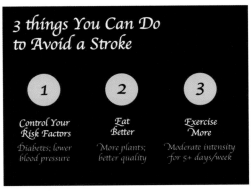

Sans serif, serif, and script fonts

the different elements on your slide (more on hierarchy in chapter 4), and to help focus your audience's attention.

You can also pair completely different fonts within your slides, which can help distinguish different elements of your slide. For example, a heavy block text like **NEUTRA DISPLAY TITLING** (a free font available from the resources listed below) can be used for titles, but is less appropriate for text, graphs, or tables in the body of your slide.

If you decide to use multiple font types, use them consistently and limit yourself to two or three—combining too many font types can be distracting and disorienting for your audience. Also, if you are going to pair multiple fonts, they need to be recognizably different; if your fonts are too similar, your audience may not realize that the change in font is intentional.

As with colors, moving away from default fonts will make your presentation more memorable. It's not that default fonts like Calibri (on Windows) and Cambria (on Mac OS) are necessarily bad fonts, it's just that *everyone* uses them. Using other fonts, even other default fonts, can give your presentation a more custom feel. As examples, default fonts such as Century Gothic, Tahoma, Trebuchet MS, and Verdana are effective for presentations and can be shared across platforms. On the Mac OS, Lucida Grande and Gill Sans MT

Pairing fonts (large, serif font in title and sans serif font in body)

Calibri
Cambria
Lucida Grande
Verdana
Trebuchet MS
Tahoma
Gill Sans MT

Other default fonts

(which are often available on the Windows operating system) are additional good choices. If you are going to present data in tables and graphs, be sure to review how the numbers will appear in your slides. There is little choice when it comes to the fonts for equations in the Microsoft Office package; symbols are typically fixed in the Cambria Math font. Other presentation tools, such as the LaTeX-based program Beamer, offer more flexibility for mathematical equations.

What constitutes a good typeface? For me, it's text that clearly shows letters and numbers, and contains visible distinctions between family types (such as regular, bold, and thin). If you want to move beyond the default fonts installed on your computer, there are many free fonts available that can be easily downloaded and installed. The slide on the next page shows some examples of free fonts that I have seen work well in presentations.

FINDING NEW FONTS

There are a number of online resources you can use to find more options. I list a few here with more available on the book's website:

Free custom fonts

GOOGLE FONTS. This no-frills site from Google has hundreds of free fonts, which you can browse with simple search and dropdown menus. Google Fonts may be your best bet when looking for free fonts. Google also allows you to enter your own text to test how it will appear in a presentation.

FONT SQUIRREL. This is a great resource with a wide array of fonts. Some are free, and some are available for purchase. The site shows you all of the different fonts within a font family (e.g. regular, bold, and thin), is clear about the licensing, and explains how to download the file(s). As with Google Fonts, you can take the font for a spin by using their "Test Drive" feature. It allows you to try out some of your text to see how it will appear in the chosen font.

MY FONTS. This site provides another good font library, with fonts mainly available for purchase. My Fonts also has a tool called "What The Font" that you can use to figure out which font is being used in an image or on a website—just upload an image, answer some questions to help identify the specific characters, and it will try to identify the font.

TYPE GENIUS. Type Genius is a great resource if you want to use multiple fonts. You can select a variety of fonts and see real examples of these different fonts paired with other fonts. The site also allows you to see what font pairs others are using.

As you consider whether to use non-standard fonts in your presentation, be forewarned that even if you insert them into your presentation they may not appear as intended on someone else's computer. The reason you can share and edit your document with a Times New Roman font on your colleague's computer is because that font is installed on both computers. Font compatibility is made even more difficult with different operating systems (Windows vs. Mac OS) and with different versions of the software.

INSTALLING FONTS

Installing fonts on your computer is fairly straightforward. Usually, you download a font family with multiple font types (for example, Avenir, Avenir Light, and **Avenir Bold**) in a compressed "zip" file format. You then need to unzip the file; double- or right-clicking on the folder should do this automatically.

On computers running Windows operating systems, double-clicking the typeface itself will launch a new window with an *Install* button at the top. Clicking that button will automatically move the files to the *Font* folder. Alternatively, you can drag-and-drop the font files to the *Font* folder; in recent versions of the Windows OS, the *Font* folder can be found via the *Control Panel*, and on the Mac OS, the *Font* folder can be located in the *Library* directory. When you download a font or a font family to your computer, you may find different file extensions in the compressed folder such as .ttf ("TrueType") and .otf ("OpenType"). You don't need to worry too much about this, as the computer's operating system will tell you which files you can use. You may need to restart your slide software tool to use the recently installed font(s). Once restarted, your new font(s) will appear in the regular *Font* menu.

In either operating system, you can uninstall the font(s) by simply deleting it from the *Font* folder.

If you are presenting using someone else's computer, or if you are trying to share your slide deck, there are a few ways to address the font compatibility problem:

1. Perhaps the easiest strategy is to save your presentation as a PDF file; PDFs usually maintain your fonts' appearance and won't vary with changing computers or operating systems. To save a PowerPoint file as a PDF, select the *Save As* option from the *File* menu and change the filename extension to PDF.
2. Another option is to provide the actual fonts in your presentation along with your slide deck to the person whose computer you will be using. The recipient can install the fonts on his or her machine, and then things should work smoothly.
3. Finally, you can try embedding the fonts in your presentation. This save option—not available on all presentation software programs—means the appearance of your fonts should be maintained on another computer. You will not be able to edit the slides on the other computer because it may not have the font. Recent versions of PowerPoint on the Windows operating system will allow you to embed the fonts by modifying the *Save* options in the *File Options* menu (PowerPoint 2011 on the Mac OS does not allow you to embed fonts in your file).

As with color, the fonts you choose can influence how your audience views and responds to your presentation, and how you direct their attention to specific elements on your slides. Choosing a nonstandard font isn't difficult—your computer likely comes with a full library of font choices that can be used effectively to give your slides a new, fresh look, and the Internet provides many more.

▶   ▶   ▶   ▶   ▶

Now that you've chosen your colors and fonts, it's time to decide what you are going to put on your slides—text, graphs and tables, and images. The next several chapters explore each of these slide elements and demonstrate ways to communicate your content using the most effective methods possible.

THREE THINGS TO REMEMBER ABOUT TYPE

1. **Visualize.** Your audience will immediately be influenced by the text on your slides. Consider your choices carefully.
2. **Unify.** Be consistent with your use of type. Select one to two fonts to use throughout your presentation.
3. **Focus.** Use larger text to allow your audience to see the items quickly and easily, so they can return to the job of paying attention to you. A minimum font size of 28 points is a good rule to follow but the specific size may vary depending on the font used.

PART TWO

BUILDING YOUR PRESENTATION

THE TEXT SLIDE

With a plan in place for color and type, it's time to work on translating your completed worksheet, outline, index cards, and Post-It Notes into an effective and engaging presentation. As you do so, be aware that every element of your slide is yet another item for your audience to try to decipher and understand, distracting their attention from what you are saying. This is especially true with text: Your audience will try to read all of the text you place on your slides. While your text can help support your point and argument, not everything you say needs to be displayed on the screen. Being more discerning about what you show, and when, will ensure your audience follows at your pace rather than jumping ahead and being bored while you catch up. This chapter shows you ways to use text carefully and strategically in your presentation to focus your audience's attention where you want it and better unify what you say with what you show.

DECLUTTER AND USE LESS TEXT

Many of us have been encouraged to pick up bad habits from our presentation software. For instance, the initial default slide type in PowerPoint invites you to create bullet point-heavy slides and to add as much content onto the slide as possible. This is ultimately to the detriment of your audience. Instead of letting the default setup determine your slide layout, I encourage you to always start with a blank slide. This will let you choose each slide element, and force you to consider exactly what you wish to include.

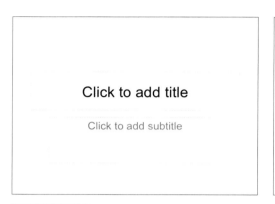

Default PowerPoint slides

Of course, PowerPoint is not solely to blame for messy, cluttered slides. Sometimes we pack our slides with text and bullet points as a reminder of the multiple things we plan to discuss. We use the text slide as a crutch to ensure we don't forget something—a kind of presentation CliffsNotes. How many times have you seen a presenter look up to a slide to make sure they've covered all of the listed bullet points?

Often we use this approach because it's the easiest, quickest way to convert our written report to slides. Each topic sentence of each paragraph in the paper becomes a bullet point

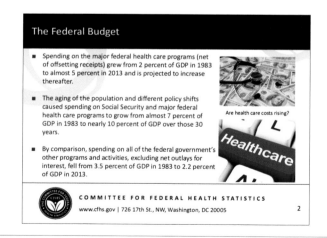

Typical slide with too much text, random images, and captions
(Data from Congressional Budget Office, 2014)

and, voilà, we're done. However, including too much text on your slides ignores the very principle of using them: slides are intended for the audience, not the presenter.

Each one of your slides should have a single goal. This will force your audience to focus on your most important points, and not allow them to become distracted by different numbers, topics, or text. For example, this slide from the fictional "Committee on Federal Health Statistics" (though based on an actual slide from a not-so fictional federal agency) has a look and layout you'll doubtlessly recognize from innumerable presentations—small title, lots of text, random images, and maybe some captions.

Two things happen when you present a slide like this, full of text and bullets:

1. **Your audience reads instead of listening.** When your audience is presented with a slide full of text, they usually follow their initial instinct to read all of it. If they're reading your slides, they're likely not listening to you. Contrary to what many people might think, we are not that good at multitasking. In fact, there is a long literature, including the book *Reading in the Brain* by Stanislas Dehaene (2009), which argues that processing verbal information as speech relies on many of the same networks in the brain as processing verbal information as text. Therefore, doing both simultaneously overloads the brain's ability to process either stream of information. Your audience cannot read your slides, listen to you, take notes, and think critically about your presentation all at once.

2. **Your audience listens to you say things they just read.** Your audience usually can read faster than you can speak. In addition, you are probably going to elaborate on certain points, so there's little doubt your audience will have read your entire slide before you are done presenting the information. Realizing what you say mirrors almost identically with what's on the screen permits your audience to quickly read the slide and then stop paying attention to you until you move on to the next slide. They now have time to check their email, think about what they need to do after your talk, or consider their dinner options. Any of these things are distractions and shift their attention away from you and your presentation. Having slides overly cluttered with information also means your audience will never be surprised. The presentation structure I recommend gives your audience a preview of your conclusions at the very beginning of your report, but unexpected statistics or counterintuitive findings can be a great way to engage the audience when you get to the details of your presentation. You can't capture the "surprise factor" if you include everything on each slide.

In this section, I urge you to change the basic habit of including as much text as possible on every slide. Instead, I suggest you follow the guiding principles outlined earlier: *focus* your audience's attention on your important points, *unify* the spoken word with the visual display, and do so in a consistent way throughout your presentation.

The very first step to creating more effective text slides is to *focus* the audience's attention on content by removing as much visual clutter as possible. Images can do important work—they can communicate information, evoke a certain mood, or subtly encourage the reader to focus on you and what you're saying rather than on the slide (we'll discuss this more in the next chapter). However, if you're including images just for the sake of having images, chances are they'll just add clutter. The same is true for including unnecessary text. Remember, not everything you say needs to go on your slide. If it's a simple, short point and you are going to just say it, you may be able to leave it off the slide altogether.

You can usually also delete the actual bullet points. Bullet points are used to separate portions of text and create hierarchy. In this case, the distance between each sentence provides that visual space, so deleting the bullet points leaves enough white space to serve equally well in separating the text. Removing such clutter will have the immediate advantage of permitting you to increase the size of the remaining text—allowing you to design for the back row.

This slide also follows the common practice of including a logo and website as part of the footer, meaning it is on every slide in the presentation. The logo takes up a significant

AVOIDING ORPHANS AND OTHER MISTAKES

Notice the dangling word "years" in the second bullet of the original Committee on Federal Health Statistics slide, disconnected from the "30." A word left dangling like this at the end of a paragraph is called an "orphan." Isolated words can be distracting for your reader, especially when (as in this case) the break comes between a number and its units. You can easily avoid this interruption in the flow of your text—and the subsequent break in the reader's focus—by resizing the text or text box.

Also remember to check your slides for typos and be consistent in your use of punctuation. If you want to use periods, use them consistently. Run a quick spellcheck on your slides. And avoid using all capital letters in your text; it is more difficult to read and people now recognize all capital letters as yelling.

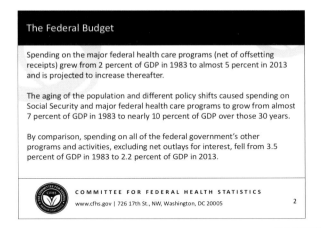

Delete the actual bullet points

amount of space, spanning the entire bottom region. It's not as if your audience will need to be reminded of where you work when you get to the fourth slide. If your organization requires you to include a logo (or disclaimer) on every slide, try to do so in a small, unobtrusive way. For instance, use just the logo rather than the logo and full organization name. You can also deemphasize the visual appearance of the logo by making it gray scale or adding a transparency. If you are not required to insert your logo on every slide, I recommend including it only on the first and last slide of your presentation. You can also safely leave out the Web address on all but your title slide—chances are your audience can find you on the Web without seeing your website on each of your forty-five slides.

Many presenters insist they or their organization prefer to have the logo on every slide so that it can be identified when the slides are printed, copied, or posted online by another person. This approach fails to recognize the difference between slides that are presented and those that are read. Presentation slides should be built for just that—presenting. If you eliminate or deemphasize logos, you can focus your audience's attention on your content and maximize the slide space with your message. Furthermore, people who post your slides online are likely to strip out the identifying branding and post only the image or content they want, so it's probably better to use the slide space for your audience regardless.

Finally, the page number serves no purpose in a spoken presentation, other than giving your audience something to look at and having them guess how many slides you have in total. Page numbers are really only necessary for handouts, not for presentation slides.

The Federal Budget

Spending on the major federal health care programs (net of offsetting receipts) grew from 2 percent of GDP in 1983 to almost 5 percent in 2013 and is projected to increase thereafter.

The aging of the population and different policy shifts caused spending on Social Security and major federal health care programs to grow from almost 7 percent of GDP in 1983 to nearly 10 percent of GDP over those 30 years.

By comparison, spending on all of the federal government's other programs and activities, excluding net outlays for interest, fell from 3.5 percent of GDP in 1983 to 2.2 percent of GDP in 2013.

Remove unnecessary footer elements

How does knowing that you are on slide 17 help your audience? These default markers take up valuable slide real estate that could be used for images, graphs, and content.

SLIDE HEADLINES

Now that you've removed the clutter, more attention can be paid to the text itself. Let's start at the top, with the headline. As noted in chapter 1, presentation author Carmine Gallo recommends using specific, memorable, concise, "Twitter-like" headlines. Headlines matter, he argues, because they "are what persuade you to read particular stories in newspapers, magazines or blogs" (47). The idea is not to "dumb down" your content, but to highlight the most important point you want your audience to consider. For instance, instead of using the nondescript phrase "Outlook for the Federal Budget" as your slide title, you can use a more active title that summarizes the content of the slide: "Federal Health Care Spending Rose Quickly." This gives your audience context for the points that are to come.

Your use of type should help guide your audience through your slides, from your headlines to your main points. With effective use of hierarchy, you can apply order to your slides and make sure your audience sees the most important items first. Randomly throwing text on a slide with different sizes and levels of emphasis can create confusion. Many presentation software tools offer the ability to add different text effects such as

**Federal Health Care Spending
Rose Quickly**

Spending on the major federal health care programs (net of
offsetting receipts) grew from 2 percent of GDP in 1983 to almost
5 percent in 2013 and is projected to increase thereafter.

The aging of the population and different policy shifts caused
spending on Social Security and major federal health care
programs to grow from almost 7 percent of GDP in 1983 to nearly
10 percent of GDP over those 30 years.

By comparison, spending on all of the federal government's other
programs and activities, excluding net outlays for interest, fell
from 3.5 percent of GDP in 1983 to 2.2 percent of GDP in 2013.

Create an active, Twitter-like headline

shadows, glow, reflections, and 3D. My best advice is to avoid these effects, as they often
appear childish, especially for scholarly presentations, and harken back to days of cheap,
low-quality design and images. Your audience will spend time trying to decipher what's
important on your slide rather than listening to you speak. To create effective slide hierarchy, identify the most important points and make those the largest, boldest features.
Move from full paragraphs or sentences to only the text your audience truly needs in

**Federal Health Care Spending
Rose Quickly**

Spending on major federal health care programs
grew from 2.0% of GDP in 1983 to 4.6% in 2013

Major health care programs plus Social Security
grew from 6.7% of GDP in 1983 to 9.5% in 2013

Spending on all other federal programs fell from
3.5% of GDP in 1983 to 2.2% in 2013

Employ good text hierarchy

order to follow you. You'll find that doing this can help you further decrease the amount of text on each slide.

There may be times when you want to draw your audience's attention to certain sections of text. This can be especially useful on the (hopefully rare) occasions where you need to show a significant amount of text—a passage, a long quotation, or maybe a question from the survey you've conducted. Proceed carefully in this case; it can be annoying having someone read to you, so as the presenter, you may want to stand silently for a moment and let your audience read the slide. Also remember that you should be designing for the back of the room, so make the text large enough for your audience to read the passage. To emphasize portions of text, you might change the text size, or add color, or add a highlight (in this

The acquisition of skills requires a regular environment, an adequate opportunity to practice, and rapid and unequivocal feedback about the correctness of thoughts and actions. When these conditions are fulfilled, skill eventually develops, and the intuitive judgments and choices that quickly come to mind will mostly be accurate.

–Daniel Kahneman, Thinking, Fast and Slow

The acquisition of skills requires a regular environment, an adequate opportunity to practice, and rapid and unequivocal **feedback about the correctness of thoughts and actions**. When these conditions are fulfilled, skill eventually develops, and the intuitive judgments and choices that quickly come to mind will mostly be accurate.

–Daniel Kahneman, Thinking, Fast and Slow

The acquisition of skills requires a regular environment, an adequate opportunity to practice, and rapid and unequivocal **feedback about the correctness of thoughts and actions**. When these conditions are fulfilled, skill eventually develops, and the intuitive judgments and choices that quickly come to mind will mostly be accurate.

–Daniel Kahneman, Thinking, Fast and Slow

The acquisition of skills requires a regular environment, an adequate opportunity to practice, and rapid and unequivocal feedback about the correctness of thoughts and actions. When these conditions are fulfilled, skill eventually develops, and the intuitive judgments and choices that quickly come to mind will mostly be accurate.

–Daniel Kahneman, Thinking, Fast and Slow

Bring attention to sections of text
(Quote from Daniel Kahneman, *Thinking, Fast and Slow*, 2013)

CONTROL YOUR TEXT SIZE

In PowerPoint, you may find your text automatically changes size when you reach the edges of the default text boxes. You can turn this *AutoFit* feature off by using the options found in the *AutoCorrect Options...* area of the *Proofing* section in the *PowerPoint Options* menu (accessible under the *File* tab). Take control of the software and make your own formatting and design decisions, instead of letting the tools and preset defaults dictate your capabilities.

> The acquisition of skills requires a regular environment, an adequate opportunity to practice, and rapid and unequivocal feedback about the correctness of thoughts and actions. When these conditions are fulfilled, skill eventually develops, and the intuitive judgments and choices that quickly come to mind will mostly be accurate.

case, adding a yellow box behind the text). You can also use arrows or other objects to draw attention to the particular point or sentence most relevant to your argument, so that your audience's focus is in the right place.

THE LAYERING APPROACH

You now have your text on your slide, and you are focusing your audience's attention on your concise, Twitter-like headline by using larger text, boldface text, colors, highlights, or maybe even a different font. Even though we've eliminated a considerable amount of clutter on your slide—by removing the various images, captions, and bullet points—there is still a good deal of text (in full sentences) remaining, which will distract your audience and keep them from directing their full attention toward you.

Let's take this further. Instead of placing so much information on a single slide, let's break it into three, separate slides. Other than very cheap computer memory, you don't pay anything for additional slides, so use them liberally. There is an unhelpful prevailing rule that

Federal Health Care Spending Rose Quickly

Spending on major federal health care programs grew from 2.0% of GDP in 1983 to 4.6% in 2013

Major health care programs plus Social Security grew from 6.7% of GDP in 1983 to 9.5% in 2013

Spending on all other federal programs fell from 3.5% of GDP in 1983 to 2.2% in 2013

Candidate to layer text

lingers in presentation advice, which states that you should have no more slides than minutes you are going to present. I couldn't disagree more. If you prepare well, practice, and appropriately time your presentation (more on these strategies later), there is no correlation between the length of your presentation and the number of slides you use.

Breaking up complex slides into groups of simpler, cleaner slides can be a very powerful way to encourage focus and integrate what you say with what your audience sees. I call this the *layering* approach. The general philosophy is to present each point—each goal—on its own. Then together, they come back to the original slide (the one that was forcing your audience to read too much). As you discuss each point and show only the relevant text, there is a limited number of words on each slide for your audience to read. Then, they can return their attention to you as you elaborate on what's being shown on the screen.

Layering is a powerful and versatile tool for focusing your audience's attention. The approach works not only for text, but for graphs as well, as we'll see in chapter 5. When you want to make a complex point, or an argument that has several steps, you can break up a single, dense slide into multiple slides. Layering your content in this way can keep your audience focused on the exact point you are trying to make, and seamlessly integrate what you're saying with what you're showing.

The simplest way to layer text is to split the original single slide into separate slides, and then make the text for the main point of each slide darker than the point that was just covered (I'll use black and gray in this example). I like to do this by creating the final slide first;

**Federal Health Care Spending
Rose Quickly**

Spending on major federal health care programs
grew from 2.0% of GDP in 1983 to 4.6% in 2013

**Federal Health Care Spending
Rose Quickly**

Spending on major federal health care programs
grew from 2.0% of GDP in 1983 to 4.6% in 2013

Major health care programs plus Social Security
grew from 6.7% of GDP in 1983 to 9.5% in 2013

**Federal Health Care Spending
Rose Quickly**

Spending on major federal health care programs
grew from 2.0% of GDP in 1983 to 4.6% in 2013

Major health care programs plus Social Security
grew from 6.7% of GDP in 1983 to 9.5% in 2013

Spending on all other federal programs fell from
3.5% of GDP in 1983 to 2.2% in 2013

Layering text

this way, I can simply recolor and delete text as necessary. In addition, it ensures consistency because all of my text will be sized correctly and will look the same from one slide to the next. An alternative approach is using animation to make your text appear sequentially. You can do this in PowerPoint using the *Animation* tool, which I discuss briefly in the Box and in more depth on the book's companion website.

POWERPOINT ANIMATION

PowerPoint's *Animation* tool enables you to make text and other slide objects appear sequentially on the slide, so that you create the appearance of multiple slides. There are over thirty different animation options in PowerPoint including swivel, fade, dissolve, blind, and checker. You don't need any of these options and you should probably just avoid them altogether; instead, simply use the *Appear* and *Disappear* options.

To animate slide objects, first select the object and then open the *Animations* tab. Once there—in this example, with the text selected—choose *Appear*. You will see a number "1" show up next to the selected object. Repeat the process for each bullet and additional numbers will appear by each section of the text. For example, when you initially present this text slide, the first bullet will appear on the screen. Clicking once will bring up the next bullet, and then again to bring up the last bullet. You can also add different styles, timing, and animations by using the various options in the sub-menus.

Outlook for the Federal Budget

Spending on the major federal health care programs (net of offsetting receipts) grew from 2 percent of GDP in 1983 to almost 5 percent in 2013 and is projected to increase thereafter.

1 The aging of the population and different policy shifts caused spending on Social Security and major federal health care programs to grow from almost 7 percent of GDP in 1983 to nearly 10 percent of GDP over those 30 years.

2 By comparison, spending on all of the federal government's other programs and activities, excluding net outlays for interest, fell from 3.5 percent of GDP in 1983 to 2.2 percent of GDP in 2013.

Applying the layering approach to this example splits the original slide into three separate slides. As the presenter, I can show the first slide—maybe give the audience a moment to read the text—and then make my additional points and arguments. Next, I can move to the second slide, again pausing to allow the audience to read, and make my arguments and points, and so on.

Some presenters worry that this layering approach makes it more difficult to circle back to an earlier slide to help answer questions because you now have more slides to flip through. My perspective is that it is preferable to focus your audience's attention going forward as you present your material, and that they will forgive you if you need to go back to answer a question.

Other presenters will try to use a kind of reverse version of layering, putting all of the text on each slide with the text that is not yet being discussed in a lighter color. They then flip from one slide to the next sequentially, darkening the text as the presentation progresses. This is in some ways even worse than the original slide construct because the audience is still inclined to try to read the entire slide, but they now have the additional challenge of reading text in a lighter color that is harder to decipher.

Federal Health Care Spending Rose Quickly

Spending on **major federal health care programs** grew from **2.0%** of GDP in 1983 to **4.6%** in 2013

Major health care programs plus Social Security grew from **6.7%** of GDP in 1983 to **9.5%** in 2013

Spending on **all other federal programs** fell from **3.5%** of GDP in 1983 to **2.2%** in 2013

Reverse layering

THE PREVIOUS LITERATURE SLIDE

One of the places where I often see far, far too much text projected on the screen is in the Previous Literature slide. When you discuss the existing body of research, try to focus your audience's attention on the references that truly matter. Far too many presenters list every author's name (and publication date) in the Reference section of their paper. Why list seventy-five names and dates if only two or three had any direct relevance to the truncated list of points you can reasonably make in your fifteen-minute conference presentation? Your audience knows—or at least suspects—there's a long literature, so you don't need to list the entire history of the field. If your audience is interested in reading the entire literature, they can comb through the References section of your paper. Layering can also be a useful strategy in this case. Instead of including all of your citations on a single slide, you can first pare down the list and then place them into groups to be shown on different slides.

LAYERING EQUATIONS

Layering can again be very useful if you give technical presentations and need to show equations or other mathematical expressions. The logic is the same: too much information at once and your audience will have difficulty following you, and be less likely to embrace your argument and message.

As with text, equations can also be layered. There are many ways to do so, ranging from layering each specific component or variable in the equation, to just layering the definitions of each equation object. For example, consider the following equation, which estimates the returns to education. Even with only three variables on the right-hand side, this slide may appear dense and be difficult for your audience to read—there are Greek letters, symbols, numbers, and definitions, all of which distract your audience. It could be especially confusing for your audience if you show a concept or equation with which they are unfamiliar.

Instead of a single slide containing the entire equation and the definitions for each term, you can layer the equation by walking your audience through the equation term by term, or show the entire equation and then layer the terms. I then take this a step further and combine the layering approach with the strategic use of text formatting by adding color to specific parts of the equation.

Estimating Returns to Education

$$lnW_i = \beta_0 + \beta_1 S_i + \beta_2 X_i + \beta_3 X_i^2 + \varepsilon_i$$

W_i = wages

S_i = years of schooling

X_i = years of experience

ε_i = residual

Typical equation slide

Estimating Returns to Education

$$lnW_i = \beta_0 + \beta_1 S_i + \beta_2 X_i + \beta_3 X_i^2 + \varepsilon_i$$

W_i = wages

Estimating Returns to Education

$$lnW_i = \beta_0 + \beta_1 S_i + \beta_2 X_i + \beta_3 X_i^2 + \varepsilon_i$$

W_i = wages

S_i = years of schooling

Estimating Returns to Education

$$lnW_i = \beta_0 + \beta_1 S_i + \beta_2 X_i + \beta_3 X_i^2 + \varepsilon_i$$

W_i = wages

S_i = years of schooling

X_i = years of experience

Estimating Returns to Education

$$lnW_i = \beta_0 + \beta_1 S_i + \beta_2 X_i + \beta_3 X_i^2 + \varepsilon_i$$

W_i = wages

S_i = years of schooling

X_i = years of experience

ε_i = residual

Layering the equation

Remember this may be the first time your audience has seen your equations, theorems or mathematical concepts. Don't feel like you necessarily have to show the most complicated version of your equations; you might be able to show a simplified version and then describe the more complex formulation. Clearly present the essential features of your model and carefully describe your notation, even elements you expect your audience to be familiar with.

FROM TEXT TO VISUALS

You can take the layering approach further by moving away from text altogether. Notice that each point on the slide we've been working with has an associated set of numbers. The subject of the first sentence is major federal health care spending; according to the slide, spending grew from about 2 percent of GDP in 1983 to almost 5 percent in 2013. Instead of writing out all of this text, what about presenting it as a graph?

Here, I've paired the active headline with a graph instead of a long sentence. This allows your audience to see this point at a glance, and by cutting down on the amount of text, your audience is encouraged to listen to you rather than reading. I've included the numbers on this chart, but there may be times when you don't want to include any labels (for example, if you are showing multiple data points or perhaps when simply visualizing the difference between the groups is more important than the exact numbers). You can do the same with

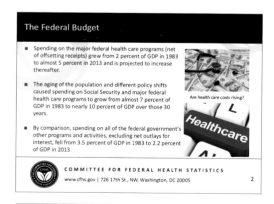
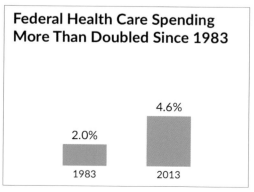

Visualize a text-dense slide

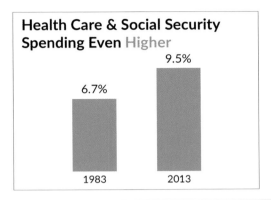

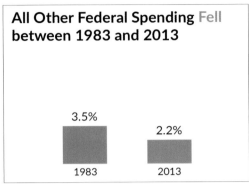

Graph each bullet point

the other two points and add them as separate slides, so that you can walk your audience through each point one at a time.

There may be times when you want your audience to focus on how something has changed, not on the data points themselves. In such cases, you can reduce the number of dimensions you show your audience by focusing on the change rather than the numbers. For example, suppose the speaker does not want to emphasize the level of health spending, Social Security spending, and all other spending, but instead chooses to highlight how these three variables have changed over the past thirty years. In this case, a column chart or a slope chart (more on these in the next chapter) might be a better approach. Also notice how both slides use the orange color to draw attention to the decline in the All Other spending category.

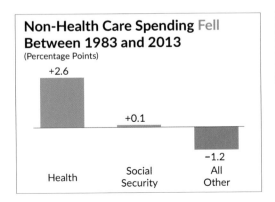

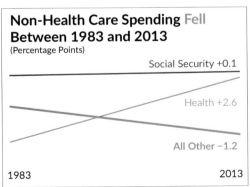

Alternative graph options

▶ ▶ ▶ ▶ ▶

Ultimately, reducing the quantity of text in your presentation will help your audience by reducing how much they need to read. If you can then replace text with visuals, and tap into our innate ability to recognize and remember images more than words, your audience will be more likely to engage with you, your presentation, and your content. How to create, find, and insert high-quality graphs, tables, and images into your presentation is the focus of the next two chapters.

THREE THINGS TO REMEMBER ABOUT THE TEXT SLIDE

1. **Visualize.** When possible, convert your text to visuals; people are more likely to remember and recognize visuals.
2. **Unify.** Maintain consistency in your text slides across your presentation by using similar layouts and structure.
3. **Focus.** Use good hierarchy and the layering technique to direct the audience's eye and draw their attention where you want it.

THE DATA VISUALIZATION SLIDE

Now that you have started considering how to effectively add text to your slides—with an eye to adding less (and larger text) to help the audience easily and quickly process it—we move on to adding visual elements. Some of the primary elements researchers will use in their presentations to show estimates and findings are graphs, charts, and other visualizations. Because, as author John Medina describes in his book *Brain Rules*, we are more likely to remember and recall information when it is presented visually, your graphs can have a profound effect on your audience, especially when they are created keeping your audience's needs in mind.

Just as many presenters give in to the temptation of PowerPoint's default settings and insert too much text into our slides, many of us have also picked up bad habits from presentation and graphing tools. In many of those tools, the default graphs include unnecessary elements and clutter. This makes it difficult for your audience or reader to clearly see the data and the specific story you are trying to tell. Instead of letting the tool tell you what graph to make and what it should look like, consider what specific message you want your graph to show. This will let you choose each gridline, tick mark, data maker, data label, color, and other objects with the audience's easy acquisition of information in mind.

There are countless ways to visualize your data including bars, lines, pies, scatterplots, and maps—the list goes on and on. Not only is it important to visualize your data when possible, but it's also good practice to be more thoughtful about the use and purpose of your data visualizations. This allows you to choose the right visual for the data and to choose the right visual for the presentation. Creating a default chart in Excel and pasting it into PowerPoint—or, worse yet, taking a blurry screenshot from your published article—ignores the fundamental difference between an image as it is read and an image as it is presented. Graphs are your opportunity to give your audience a quick, visual snapshot of your content. They should be clear, intuitive, and comprehensive so your audience can quickly process the information and return their focus to you.

USING PREATTENTIVE ATTRIBUTES

Effective data visualization taps into the brain's "preattentive visual processing," a fact perhaps first described by psychologist Anne Treisman and further applied to data visualization by a number of authors. Because our eyes detect a limited set of visual characteristics (such as shape and contrast), we combine various characteristics of an object and unconsciously perceive them as comprising an image. In contrast to "attentive processing"—the conscious part of perception that allows us to perceive and order things sequentially—preattentive processing is done in parallel with seeing. In other words, our initial perception of the object, how we focus our attention on the object, and the comparison of that object to descriptions held in memory are all done simultaneously. Thus, preattentive processing is much faster than attentive processing.

A simple example demonstrates how preattentive processing works: Count the occurrences of the number 3 in the following set.

    12695485236123569987458245
    0124036985702069568312781
    2439862012478136982173256

Now repeat the task with the next set of numbers.

    12695485236123569987458245
    0124036985702069568312781
    2439862012478136982173256

Try this set.

1269548523612356987458245

0124036985702069568312781

2439862012478136982173256

What about this set?

1269548523612356987458245

0124036985702069568312781

2439862012478136982173256

The instances of 3 in the second, third, and fourth sets are easier to find because the numbers are encoded using a different preattentive attribute. In order, color (red), intensity of
the color (gray and black), and width of the line (boldface) are used. Each distinction helps
us effortlessly identify the number 3 in the respective sets. In other words, preattentive attributes are those shapes, colors, or other effects that seem to pop out from their surroundings.

There are many preattentive attributes that tap into our eye-brain system including shape,
position, orientation, color, and width (Christopher Healey and James Enns [2012] have

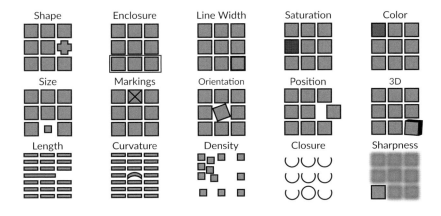

Attributes of preattentive processing

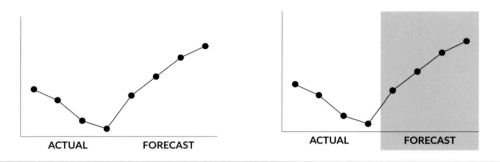

Preattentive attributes position and enclosure

demonstrations and additional examples in their paper and an online companion). You can use these attributes when presenting your data to help your audience quickly and easily grasp your meaning.

Two good examples are line charts and bar charts. A line chart uses the position of the points to indicate the data, while a bar chart uses length. You can use other preattentive attributes to draw your audience's attention to aspects of your graphs or slides, guiding their focus. In the example above, I can use the enclosure attribute to mark the *Forecast* area of the chart. Notice how the gray box immediately draws your eye to that area in particular.

Using too many of these effects, however, can undermine their collective impact. Notice how the bubble chart below employs color, position, and size to present the data. In the figure on the left, the eye moves all over because it's not clear what color or bubble size demands attention. When some of the bubbles are changed to a nondescript gray color, you suddenly find yourself focusing on the group of red bubbles and the lonely blue bubble.

Preattentive attributes position, size, and color

As you create your graphs, consider what you want your audience to focus on and use some of these preattentive attributes to more effectively visualize your data and focus their attention. You can also use the three basic principles from chapter 1 to guide your use and creation of data visualizations:

1. **Visualize.** This one is self-explanatory, right? *Show* your results, and don't just say them. Definitely do not leave them in bullet points or in complex, impossible-to-read tables with 20 columns and 40 rows. Your presentation is not the time to go into every detail of your analysis, but it is an opportunity to highlight the important aspects and findings. Visualizing the key elements will make them clearer and more memorable for your audience. Think of it this way: Which is easier, describing a circle in words or showing one on a screen?

2. **Unify.** Use graph types, colors, and fonts that match the aesthetic and layout of the rest of your presentation. Having a unified set of visuals shows your audience that you considered their overall experience and how best to present your work. Resist the temptation to verbally narrate your graphs, spelling out the details of every element of each and every visualization. Instead, merge text, graphs, and the spoken word, all with the singular goal of effective communication. This also means combining text and graphs instead of leaving them disconnected: Move your legends—often placed off to the side or below the graph—directly onto your graph or below the title. You can reduce the amount of mental effort your audience needs to expend by integrating the graph and the text, so they can quickly turn their attention back to you as you speak.

3. **Focus.** The detailed, specific graph in your written paper may give your reader a great deal of information, but you will lose your audience if you put the same graph on a screen. Researchers tend to place too much clutter on their graphs: dark or heavy gridlines; unnecessary tick marks, labels, and text; nonessential icons or pictures; ornamental shading and gradients; and purposeless dimensions. These elements can distract your audience and may distort your presentation of the data.

Creating better, more effective visualizations for research presentations (line charts, bar charts, area charts, maps, etc.) does not require expensive software tools or weeks-long training, but it does require thoughtful consideration about what kind of information can and should be communicated visually—something many researchers are not used to thinking about. This chapter will focus on helping you create better visuals, so that your audience can more clearly comprehend your argument and message.

LAYERING GRAPHS

The layering principle introduced in the last chapter can be used to make almost any type of visualization easier for the audience to understand and follow. Happily, as we saw in its application to text, layering doesn't require much design skill beyond what you use to create the graph in the first place. First, you need to adjust the original graph to make it easier for your audience to see the data on the screen. Then, sequentially remove objects so that each slide shows one less variable or data element. You'll now have a series of slides that gradually build to the final graph. When you present, you'll show the slides so that the audience focuses on one variable at a time as you introduce it.

Consider the *Trends in College Pricing 2015* report from The College Board, which catalogs prices charged by colleges and universities. The report contains dozens of graphs, primarily in the form of column and bar charts, line charts, and pie charts. Along with the PDF version of the report, the College Board also provides PowerPoint slides and Excel files with the raw data on their website.

First, let's look at an image provided in the written report.

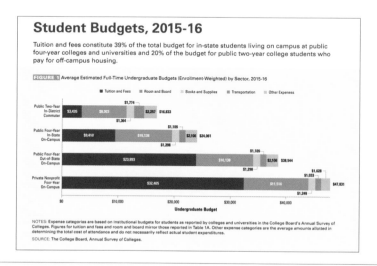

Figure 1 from *Trends in College Pricing* report.
(*Trends in College Pricing 2015*. Copyright ©2015. The College Board.
www.collegeboard.org. Reproduced with permission.)

Certainly, there are things one could improve such as directly labeling the graph instead of including a legend isolated from the data. The explanatory text above the graph emphasizes the percentage distribution of spending for students, but the graph shows dollar amounts. Clearly, the reader can make these calculations, but the headline message should match the presentation of the data. Also notice how easy it is to compare the *Tuition and Fees* category across the four sectors because they are all left aligned. It's much more difficult to compare the other categories with certainty because they are not aligned along a single baseline. Breaking the different groups apart and putting them on their own separate vertical baseline would resolve this ambiguity.

So while this chart may not be ideal, because it's in the written report the reader has time to examine the numbers in detail, investigate the different groups and bar segments, and read the labels. They can take as much time as they want to understand and process the information.

Now consider the image provided by the College Board in their PowerPoint file. There are minor differences between this image and the report version: the background color is now white instead of tan; the title is bigger; there is now a title and logo banner across the bottom; and the "Notes" are gone, as are the vertical gridlines. The content of the actual chart

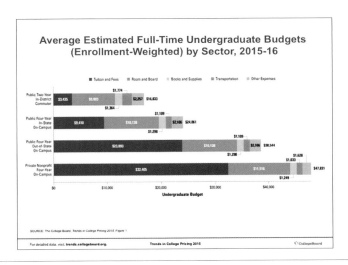

PowerPoint slide of Figure 1 (*Trends in College Pricing 2015*. Copyright ©2015.
The College Board. www.collegeboard.org. Reproduced with permission.)

remains unchanged, and the dollar labels and axis labels are still in place (all at about a 10 point font). Imagine trying to read this chart as a member of the audience. Your attempt to quickly comprehend the different budget types and categories within the bars is confounded by the different labels and small type, and your focus constantly disrupted by the speaker describing it aloud.

How can layering create a better presentation of this graph?

Remember the key to layering is to focus your audience's attention on the point you are trying to make. Let's say you're doing a presentation on the true cost of college, and your headline message is "Better educating incoming students (and their families) on the full cost of college will boost graduation rates." You start this particular section of your presentation by making the exact point in the College Board report: There is a fairly large difference in the share of students' total budgets spent on "tuition and fees" between those attending public four-year in-state colleges and living on-campus, and those attending two-year colleges and living off-campus. Next, you want to focus in greater detail on the former group, and examine the constraints on their remaining budget.

This is where unification between what you're saying and what you're showing comes in: How will you talk about this point, and what parts of the graph will best supplement your discussion? Figuring out how you would like to move the audience through a particular graph is the first step in determining how you'll layer it.

For this example, you might divide the single slide into five, separate slides. First, you can show just the *Tuition and Fees* values for the four categories, highlighting the values for the two different types of students you're examining. In the next slide, by turning your focus to other costs, you can show the values for *Room and Board*, perhaps now focusing just on the in-state on-campus students. Notice how separating these segments onto their own vertical axis makes it easier to compare costs across the four categories. Similar to layering with text, graying out the bars from the previous slide will help the audience focus on the spending type of interest. Also note that in this example, I've changed the metric from dollars to percentages to better match the proportions story. In addition, I've strategically placed the five icons above each set of bars. This minor design addition reminds your audience what previous categories were without cluttering the slide with more text (more information about where to find and how to insert icons and images is discussed in the next chapter).

By simplifying the graph and making both it and the text larger, you've made it easier for your audience to quickly absorb the data, and then turn their attention back to you.

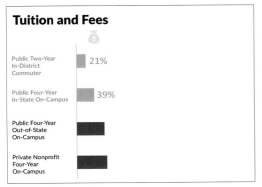

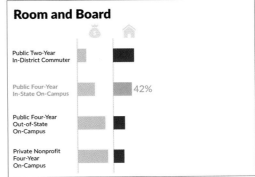

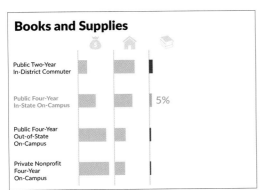

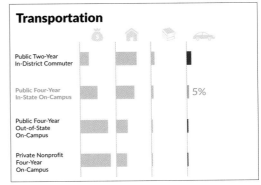

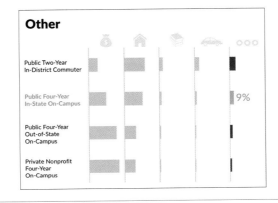

Remaking, simplifying, and layering the original College Board graph

BAR AND COLUMN CHART LABELS

There are times when you might have long x-axis labels that don't fit into the slide space. Consider how difficult it is to decipher the College Board graph if it is a stacked column chart with labels rotated 90 degrees (an approach that is far too common). Most software programs will rotate axis labels in this way to fit them into the available space, which forces your reader or audience to turn their heads sideways. Instead of worrying about changing the font size or rotating the text to fit within the space, you will usually be better off simply rotating the data and creating a horizontal bar chart. We still perceive the data based on the length of the bars, but now the labels are much easier to read.

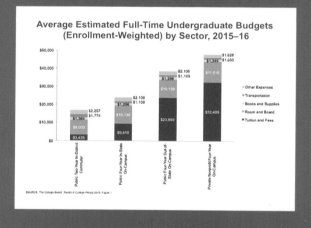

If your presentation is on students' college budget as a whole, you may feel that it's crucial for your audience to see this all in one place—that is to see the original, dense graph. However, even in this case, you can still go though each sector one at a time, using the layering approach to introduce each category, and then come back to the full graph at the end. Since the reader has already been provided with each detail, they are now comfortable with focusing on the bigger picture. An alternative strategy, particularly if you're in a small enough group, is to provide the graph as a handout. You can then stand quietly for a moment while the audience reads the material they have in front of them.

Once they've finished, you can discuss the graph with the audience's undivided attention. However, this approach can be tricky; if you provide the handout at the beginning of the presentation, you run the risk that the audience will read it while you are speaking. I discuss effective strategies for using handouts, and the pros and cons of doing so, in chapter 9.

In general, the layering strategy is easy to implement and follows the same techniques used with text. Create the last graph first, and make sure you have *everything* in place, including the titles, data labels, and axes. You can then duplicate the graph and start removing items or turning the color to match the background color of your slides.

When making your graphs, be sure to lock the axis scales first to ensure the bars or lines don't shift. In other words, you want your axes to remain consistent across the graphs. In the example below, the dark blue bars show the same values in the two graphs, but look very different when the vertical axis range changes from 0–20 percent to 0–40 percent. If you create your graphs in PowerPoint, you can also use the Animation tab to make different series *Appear* or *Disappear*. Tutorials on how to do so can be found on the book's website.

You may have noticed a major change between the original College Board image and my revisions—in general there is much less text. Your audience can better understand and extract value from your visualizations if you reduce the amount of text and labels you put on the slide and just state the information instead. For example, rather than including labels on your axes, you could simply define the graph for your audience as you present.

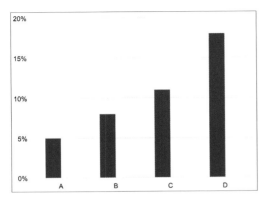 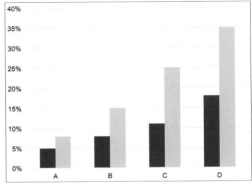

Fix the vertical axis to make sure the data are presented consistently from slide to slide

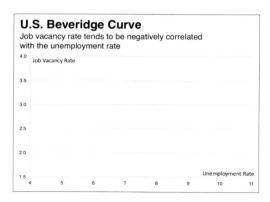

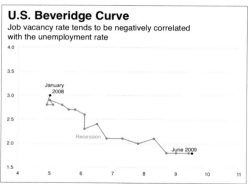

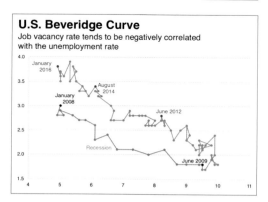

First show axes, then content
(Data from Bureau of Labor Statistics, 2016a,b)

Another strategy you can use is to first show *just* the axes. When you add your data to the chart in the second step (and continue to layer—with the third slide in this example), your audience knows how the graph space is defined. They can then process the content of the graph and the message given the data.

Other text you may be able to do without is the long list of sources and notes at the bottom of the slide. If the details are important enough, you can say them aloud, but including full, long, detailed sources and notes (oftentimes with an URL) becomes distracting clutter that your audience may try to read instead of listening to you. This isn't to say there isn't a place for a short "Source: Census Bureau" text box at the bottom of the slide or a legend for the asterisks denoting statistical significance (though you could just as well define them aloud). Attribution is important, as I'll discuss in the next chapter on images; however, you usually don't need to include the full title of the paper and data source on every graph and table. Instead, consider adding a slide at the end of your presentation that includes all this content, and the related details—an "endnote" slide, if you will. Here you can list the information for the slides that need it in a single location. This is not typically a slide you would show during your presentation, but if you plan to share your slides you can let people know that it's included. Even if you don't plan to circulate your presentation, you will have this "endnote" slide already prepared for people who might request a specific source or other detail.

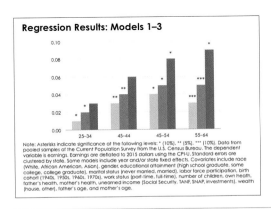

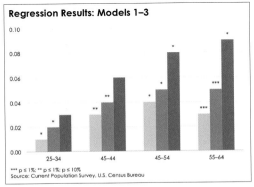

Cutting or reducing unnecessary sources and notes

DATA VISUALIZATION BOOKS

If you want to learn more about data visualization, there are some great books that dive deeper into the discussion of data visualization. Additional books, blogs, and other resources are listed on the book's website. Some of the best are listed below.

Alberto Cairo. Author of two books on data visualization, *The Functional Art* and *The Truthful Art*, with a third coming out in another year or two. Cairo is a journalism professor, so his books focus primarily on creating data visualizations for telling stories to a wide audience. The books provide fundamental overviews of data, data visualization, introductory statistics, and how to create visualizations.

Jorge Camões. His book *Data at Work* covers a wide range of data visualization principles and strategies, ranging from rules of visual perception to design considerations to data preparation and visualization.

Stephanie Evergreen. Author of two books on data visualization, her latest, *Effective Data Visualization: The Right Chart for the Right Data* is an introductory look at data visualization and a step-by-step guide to creating a variety of graphs in Excel.

Stephen Few. Author of several books on data visualization, his *Show Me the Numbers* and *Now You See It: Simple Visualization Techniques for Quantitative Analysis* are comprehensive overviews of how to present data effectively and strategically.

Isabel Meirelles. A professor of design, Meirelles' *Design for Information* surveys current examples of data visualizations for both elements of content and design. Numerous examples provide a library of visualization types and approaches.

Andy Kirk. Author of two books on data visualization, his latest, *Data Visualisation: A Handbook for Data Driven Design* provides readers with a system to conceptualize and develop data visualizations, and a process to help readers make design choices that result in clear and effective visualizations.

Cole Nussbaumer Knaflic. Knaflic's book *Storytelling with Data*, and blog of the same name, provides an introductory treatment of data visualization, and how to pair text with graphs to tell effective, compelling stories.

Edward Tufte. Tufte's four self-published books are classics in the field of data visualization. His *The Visual Display of Quantitative Information* is especially relevant to introductory data visualization including various examples and techniques.

Dona Wong. Wong's *Guide to Information Graphics* dedicates individual pages to specific graph types, how and why to choose the best chart to fit the data, the most effective way to communicate data, and what to include and not include in different graphs.

BASIC CHART REDESIGNS: LINE CHARTS

Poor graphs communicate ineffectively, or even worse, provide a distorted impression of the data. In this section, I demonstrate how to think more strategically about visualizing your data and present some pathways to create better, more effective graphs. You can construct all kinds of graphs using nothing more complicated than Excel.

Many graphs created for use in papers and reports show too much information. When they're used as is in presentations, your audience will have a hard time seeing the details and knowing where to focus. Their attention will be divided, and they'll end up distracted while you speak.

Consider the following graph from the Social Security Advisory Board. Having so many lines crossing one another (not to mention the unnecessary border that frames the entire graph) makes it difficult to see any single trend or pattern. These so-called "spaghetti charts" can be even more tangled; we've all seen graphs with so many lines and data that it's impossible to comprehend what's being shown. Even with only four lines, this graph has shortcomings: The crossing of the lines, in addition to the data markers on every point, make it hard to focus on any single pattern. The legend is located off to the side, rather than being unified within the graph. Sadly, the default Excel 2010 colors suggest the author did not unify these colors with other elements of the presentation, and gave little thought to whether these choices would sufficiently convey the information.

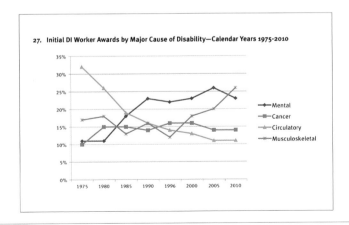

Spaghetti line chart of Disability Insurance awards, by cause of disability
(Source: Social Security Advisory Board, 2012)

A good presentation of this chart could show each of the four lines separately, an easy and natural way to layer. You could also lighten the gridlines and perhaps eliminate the percentage signs along the y-axis by adding a "(Percent)" subtitle. Finally, integrating the legend with the data allows you to increase the size of the graph on the slide, which makes it easier for your audience to link the labels and data.

There are several strategies you can use to present a complicated line chart to your audience. The first strategy is to layer, sequentially presenting each series on a single chart. As you speak, highlight each individual series, but leave the other series on the graph. Then your audience can easily see the *relative* patterns of all of your data. Notice how the blue lines stand out against the gray lines sitting in the background, which provide a frame of reference. The layering approach is a good way to show the reader the different pieces of a

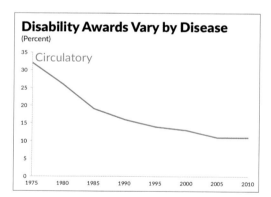

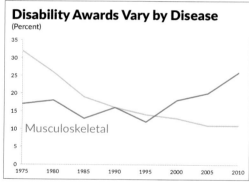

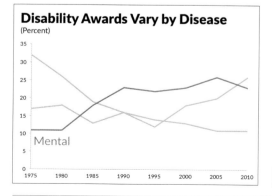

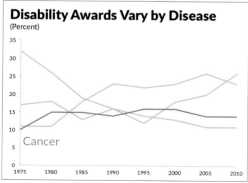

Layering a single chart one series at a time

larger picture. It is also perhaps the simplest approach because you just repeat and modify the original, more complex graph.

Another strategy is to take the "small multiples" approach. With small multiples, you create multiple, small versions of the graph. For presentations, you can use small multiples with a layering approach, by sequentially adding each additional graph. When I use the small multiples approach—creating graphs in either Excel or PowerPoint—I usually begin by making the last graph first. (Make sure the minimum and maximum values of the y-axis are locked, because the software may change the axis once you start deleting different data series.) Aligning the charts in PowerPoint is easy to do by using the *Format* menu to set the height and width of the chart, and then using the *Arrange* menu to align the charts together on the slide.

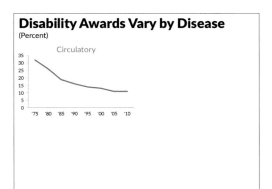

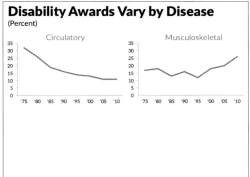

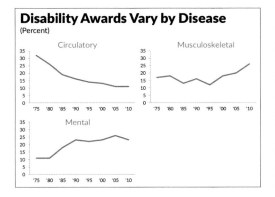

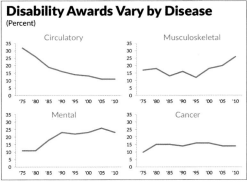

Using small multiples to layer the graph

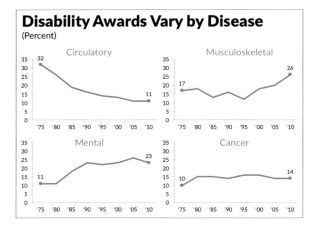

Adding data markers to small multiples

With the additional space on the slide afforded by integrating the legend and breaking the chart apart, you could also add some data values. Although doing so adds text to the slide, if you are planning on mentioning specific values, this will reinforce these numbers for the audience and will be an aid to you—you won't need to rely on your memory or notes.

If you feel that the patterns are simple enough for your audience to understand without walking them through each series—say, for instance, your chart just shows several lines that run parallel to one another—then you may decide not to break up the graphs or layer at all. In

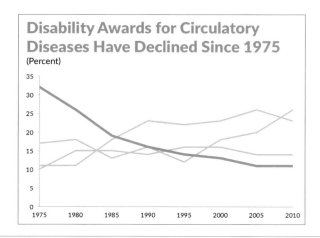

Highlighting a single data series and linking to the slide headline

these cases, try to give your audience a moment to absorb the basic patterns before you start speaking. Remember, if you show too much information on your slides, your audience will have difficulty extracting the meaning of a single series or drawing an overall conclusion. If you really only want to focus on a single story or data series, you can direct your audience's attention by highlighting that particular line and adding a more descriptive, active title. You might then simply mention what each line represents without going into detail on the remaining series.

BASIC CHART REDESIGNS: THE CLUTTERPLOT

You can apply the same techniques to more complicated graphs such as scatterplots. This scatterplot—which I affectionately call a clutterplot—makes a regular appearance in research reports and in conference and seminar presentations. Constructed in the Stata statistical package—with no changes to the default layout, font, or labels—this kind of slide shows the audience that the presenter has given little if any thought to effectively presenting their data and evidence.

Suppose you're discussing the relationship between the gross domestic product (GDP) per capita and life expectancy for a cluster of five countries: Japan, Norway, Russia, Switzerland, and the United States. Hats off to audience members who know the three-letter codes for these five countries—but even if they do, good luck finding them in the haystack of labels

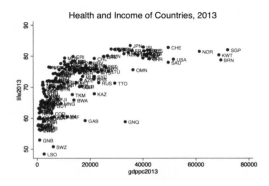

Default "clutterplot" (created in Stata) showing relationship between per capita gross domestic product and life expectancy (Data from Gapminder, 2016)

and dots. A chart like this would be difficult to decipher even in written form; in presentation form, it's hopeless. Establishing the principles of focusing, visualizing, and unifying can help you create a better visualization.

First, focus. Emphasizing the five identified countries and de-emphasizing the rest will go a long way toward demonstrating how this visualization reinforces your point. Next, visualize the data of interest for your audience, accomplished here by using a different, highlighting color. Finally, to achieve a unified look, change the color palette and font to match the rest of your presentation. Unifying the type across the text and graphs will help emphasize the coherence of your overall argument. Finally, you want to make sure that all the text is easily readable—use full words instead of mysterious abbreviations, and avoid vertical text where possible.

Once you've simplified and clarified your presentation of the data, think about the headline that will best serve your purpose. If your goal is to simply share this information or talk about the sample being used in the analysis, you may want to go with something neutral, such as the headline on the left. However, if you have a specific goal—say, to discuss the position of the United States relative to the rest of the sample—you can use a more active title to help support your specific point or argument, as shown on the right.

It is possible, of course, that some audience members will want to find other individual countries or identify various outliers, in which case you can simply refer them to the original paper or data set. Your purpose in showing this type of graph is to compare specific data points, so you want to visually emphasize these points for your audience. Your presentation is not the time for offloading all of your data onto your slides for your audience to sort through.

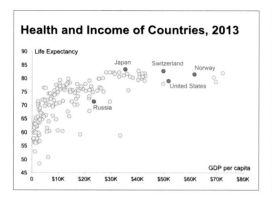 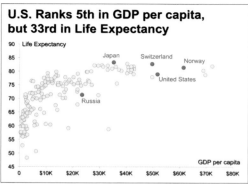

Focusing attention on countries of interest with neutral or active titles

BASIC CHART REDESIGNS: THE PIE CHART

From lines and scatterplots, we turn to pies. The debate concerning the effectiveness of pie charts is among the most contentious in the field of data visualization (much of the discussion in this section is based on Stephen Few's, "Save the Pies for Dessert"). Many people love pie charts—they are familiar, easily understood, and present "part-to-whole" relationships in an obvious way. Because pie charts force the viewer to make comparisons using the area of the slices or the angles formed by the slices—something our visual perception does not accurately support—many argue that they are not an effective way to communicate information. Donut charts, where the center of the pie is removed, just exacerbate the problem. The empty center makes the audience *estimate* the angle, and arrive at other qualitative part-to-whole judgments without being able to see the center where the edges meet. (Recent research by Robert Kosara and Drew Skau suggests that we perceive the quantities of the slices of pie or donut charts not through angle, but through area or arc length.)

Pie chart slices forming 90-degree right angles—slices that form one-quarter increments—are the ones most familiar to our eyes. Other angle dimensions can be far more difficult to discern. For example, in the pie chart on the left, Group C is easily identified as being about 25 percent of the whole. However, if, as in the pie chart on the right, the order of the segments is positioned so that the largest starts at the twelve o'clock position, then the value of Group C is not as easily comprehended. In this example, one small change changes our perception of the information.

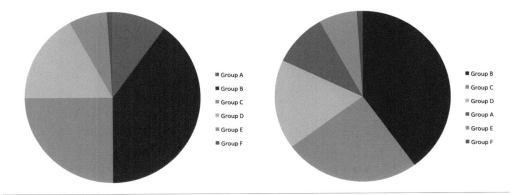

Perception of the values in the pie chart change with the orientation of the data

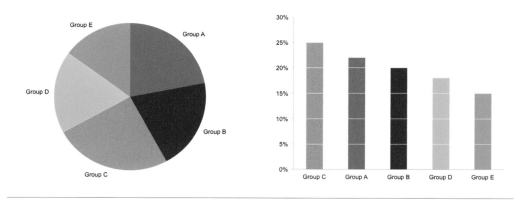

It's easier to rank values when the data are presented as a column chart

Pie charts can be especially problematic when the data values are similar. Note how difficult it is to rank the five slices from largest to smallest for the pie chart above. This is much easier when the data are presented as a bar or column chart.

Bar and column charts also only require a single color rather than multiple colors, which reduces the number of dimensions your audience needs to consider when viewing the slide. As an added bonus, it makes it easier for you as the designer because you only need a single color. This permits more flexibility in your use of color to focus the audience's attention on a particular value.

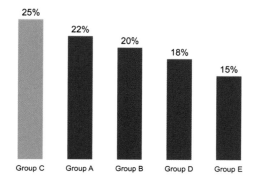

Using a column chart simplifies your color palette

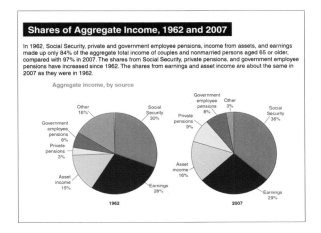

Pairs of pie charts (Source: Social Security Administration, 2009)

Even more difficult than discerning information from a single pie chart is discerning information from two pie charts. Consider the above figure from the Social Security Advisory Board. It requires the audience to figure out the difficult comparison of a large number of segments both within and between the two charts. Notice that the pie chart for 1962 has a small, unlabeled gap remaining at the twelve o'clock position. Pie charts always need to sum to 100 percent: For the redesigned graphs, I add the missing 2 percent to the "Other" category.

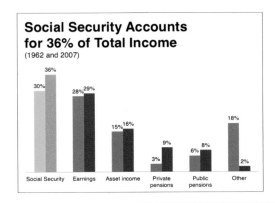

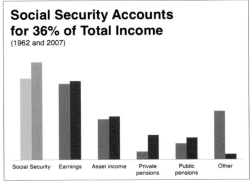

A paired column chart is a good alternative to a pair of pie charts; whether you include labels depends on your data and your message

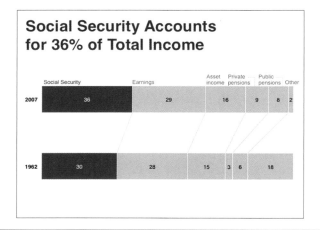

A pair of stacked bar charts is another alternative to the paired pie chart

One good alternative is the paired column chart, as shown on the previous page. Notice how even in a version without the data labels, you can still easily see the change in shares between the two years. The active headline and the yellow color for the Social Security category unify the message of the slide. If you're worried about the part-to-whole comparison, you can incorporate some descriptive language into the graph title, simply *say* the values are shares of the total, or use a stacked bar or column chart, as shown above.

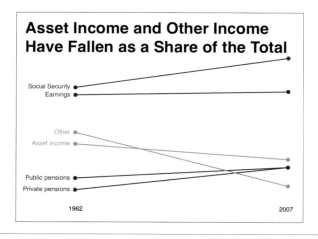

The slope chart is yet another alternative to the paired pie chart

Another alternative to the paired pie chart is a *slope chart,* which is essentially a line chart with the two categories on separate vertical axes (in this case, 1962 is on the left axis and 2009 is on the right axis). The slope chart helps you emphasize the change in the values for the different series. In this example, the use of color helps identify which categories increased over time (blue) and those that declined (orange). Notice there are no numbers on this graph. If, as presenter, you are more concerned in demonstrating how a series changed over time than with the exact numbers, this is a good approach. You can say the specific values aloud if needed, instead of putting them directly on the slide. Remember, not everything you intend to say needs to go on the screen.

Our eyes and brains are more familiar with the lengths or heights formed by bars or columns than with the segments in pie charts. Bar and column charts give a clearer picture of both the absolute amounts and the relative differences between groups. While labeling the segments of a pie chart can help clarify the exact values, requiring labels to make it legible defeats the very purpose of the chart, which is to provide a visual representation of the data.

BASIC CHART REDESIGNS: 3D CHART

I want to mention 3D charts only to strenuously encourage you not to use them. It's unfortunate that many of our software tools allow us to create things that do such a poor job visualizing data. Perhaps none is more inept than the now familiar 3D effect. It may look

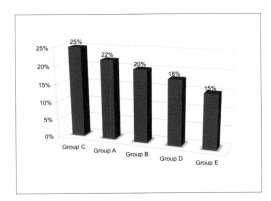
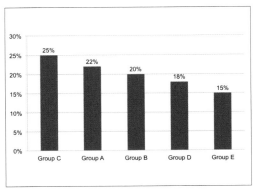

Adding 3D will often distort the presentation of the data

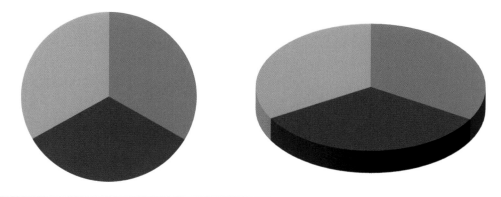

The front slice of a 3D pie chart takes up a higher proportion of the page or screen

cool, but because the third dimension does not plot data values, it just adds clutter and often distorts the data.

Remember how changing a pie chart to a column chart enabled you to better discern the quantities? I modified it on the previous page to add the 3D perspective. If you look at the 20 percent column for Group B, you'll see that no point of the column touches the gridline for that value. I've included gridlines in the 2D representation so you can see how the data are accurately represented in the 2D view. Most software tools use perspective to give depth to the imaginary plane that runs across the top of the column intersecting the gridline. So while the column label says 20 percent, your audience is going to initially view the value as something less than that amount.

A similar distortion occurs when you create 3D pie charts. In the 2D representation of this pie chart, each slice of the pie accounts for one-third of the screen. When the chart is rotated, the front slice takes up a larger proportion of the screen, thereby distorting the representation of the data.

TABLE SLIDES

As mentioned, your audience is more likely to recognize and recall information when it is presented visually. But there are times when you may want to show a dense table of numbers or results. Used carefully, tables can be a useful part of your presentation, but remember,

Table 5. Ordinary Least Squares Regression Results

	Model 1	Model 2	Model 3	Model 4
Age	-0.0431	-0.0119	-0.0207	0.0145
	[0.0216]*	[0.006]*	[0.0104]*	[0.0073]*
Gender	-0.0321	0.0138	-0.0254	0.0425
	[0.0268]	[0.0115]	[0.0212]	[0.0213]*
Experience	-0.0285	0.0265	-0.0387	0.0332
	[0.0095]***	[0.0133]**	[0.0194]**	[0.0166]*
Earnings	-0.0113	0.0287	-0.0420	0.0281
	[0.0038]***	[0.0096]***	[0.014]***	[0.021]
High School Graduate	0.0003	0.0043*	-0.0030	0.0133
	[0.0051]	[0.0026]	[0.0024]	[0.0191]
Some College	-0.0191***	-0.0066***	-0.0069***	-0.0158
	[0.0053]	[0.0025]	[0.0027]	[0.0185]
College Graduate	-0.0194***	-0.0091***	-0.0043	0.0073
	[0.0070]	[0.0033]	[0.0035]	[0.0242]
Race	0.0162***	0.0092***	0.0024	0.0238
	[0.0050]	[0.0023]	[0.0025]	[0.0154]
Ethnicity	-0.0179***	-0.0002	-0.0125***	-0.0149
	[0.0046]	[0.0022]	[0.0024]	[0.0170]
Region	0.0234***	0.0082**	0.0069*	-0.0202
	[0.0075]	[0.0037]	[0.0037]	[0.0260]
Own Home	-0.0048	-0.0023	-0.0013	-0.0218
	[0.0067]	[0.0033]	[0.0032]	[0.0215]
Smoker	-0.0058	-0.0036	0.0001	-0.0291
	[0.0050]	[0.0024]	[0.0026]	[0.0181]
Married	0.0122**	0.0053**	0.0029	0.0429**
	[0.0053]	[0.0024]	[0.0029]	[0.0173]
Widowed	-0.0285***	-0.0189***	-0.0022	-0.0397**
	[0.0060]	[0.0034]	[0.0028]	[0.0201]
Number of Children	-0.0019	0.0008	-0.0034	0.0088
	[0.0078]	[0.0036]	[0.0041]	[0.0256]
Social Security Income	-0.0120	-0.0278***	0.0004	-0.0238
	[0.0082]	[0.0066]	[0.0032]	[0.0270]
Disability Income	-0.0257***	-0.0170***	-0.0062**	-0.0491**
	[0.0068]	[0.0041]	[0.0030]	[0.0231]
Veteran Status	-0.0058	-0.0049***	0.0012	-0.0111
	[0.0039]	[0.0019]	[0.0020]	[0.0134]
Number of Observations	24,228	24,228	24,228	4,046

Source: Author's calculations based on census data.
* significant at the 10% level, ** significant at the 5% level, *** significant at the 1% level

The typical, dense table slide of regression coefficients (not actual results)

every number, object, and shape you show on the screen is another thing your audience will process instead of concentrating on what you're saying.

Consider the descriptive measures, summary statistics, and regression results that most researchers are used to showing in a table. Indeed, when you're preparing your research for a paper, this is often the best approach. However, the 40-row, 10-column regression table included in your written report is probably not going to show up very well on a projector in front of 50 people. Tables in general are difficult to use in a presentation setting, because the purpose of a table is to show detailed, actual values.

Even our standby solutions—giving the audience a moment or two of silence to absorb the information or layering the columns slide by slide—don't really work in this case. Will your audience really be able to go through the table, row by row and column by column, extracting the information pertinent to your argument? Handouts are possible, but they probably would not work with a large audience or one with mixed levels of familiarity with the material.

What about the layering technique we used for text and graphs? Applying the technique here would mean splitting this table into four separate slides. As you can see, this doesn't really help. There is still too much information for your audience to grasp.

Layering the typical table of regression coefficients—a "halfway" approach

Table 5. Ordinary Least Squares Regression Results

	Model 1	Model 2	Model 3	Model 4
Age	-0.0431	-0.0119	-0.0207	0.0145
	[0.0216]*	[0.006]*	[0.0104]*	[0.0073]*
Gender	-0.0321	0.0138	-0.0254	0.0425
	[0.0268]	[0.0115]	[0.0212]	[0.0213]*
Experience	-0.0285	0.0265	-0.0387	0.0332
	[0.0095]***	[0.0133]**	[0.0194]**	[0.0166]*
Earnings	-0.0113	0.0287	-0.0420	0.0281
	[0.0038]***	[0.0096]***	[0.014]***	[0.021]
Number of Observations	24,228	24,228	24,228	4,046

Reducing the typical table to focus on the most important numbers

A better approach to presenting detailed information is to rethink your table alto-gether. Carefully consider which numbers will help you convince your audience (without biasing their understanding or perception of your work) of the value and importance of your results—and just show those. If you are sharing a set of results that include some estimates not central to your story (for example, monthly dummy variables in a regression model), leave them out of your presentation. Just as with the headline for your overall presentation, figure out the headline message of your detailed data, and then decide how best to present it.

One alternative to a huge table is to show only the most important variables, the ones that help best convey your content, story, and conclusions, as in the slide above.

Even when condensed to just the more crucial information, this table still doesn't follow some of our other presentation guidelines, such as keeping the text big enough for those at the back of the room and keeping the formatting clean to enhance audience focus. Plus, the combination of parentheses, brackets, and asterisks makes it difficult for the reader to zero in on the most meaningful information.

As with text slides, tables should be free of clutter and have hierarchy. Use bold font or color in the column or row headers to designate them as the "titles" of the table. Also, make sure the alignment on all rows and columns is uniform. I prefer to center the text vertically within each cell, but the horizontal alignment will vary depending on the data type—for example, you should align the decimals so your audience's eyes do not have to jump around

Regression Results				
	Model 1	Model 2	Model 3	Model 4
Age	-0.0431*	-0.0119*	-0.0207	0.0145
Gender	-0.0321	0.0138	-0.0254	0.0425*
Experience	-0.0285***	0.0265**	-0.0387**	0.0332*
Earnings	-0.0113***	0.0287***	-0.0420***	0.0281*
No. of Obs.	24,228	24,228	24,228	24,228

Regression Results				
	Model 1	Model 2	Model 3	Model 4
Age	-0.0431	-0.0119	-0.0207	0.0145
Gender	-0.032	0.0138	-0.0254	0.0425
Experience	-0.0285	0.0265	-0.0387	0.0332
Earnings	-0.0113	0.0287	-0.0420	0.0281
No. of Obs.	24,228	24,228	24,228	24,228

Redesigning the table to help the audience focus on the most important numbers.
You can use color to highlight statistical significance.

from cell to cell. Where you can round the numbers, do so. Not every statistic or result needs to be accurate to the thousandths place. You might also try using color to highlight a particularly interesting result or indicate statistical significance, as with the slide on the right. Here, you can simply say, "the darkest cells here are those that are statistically significant at the 1 percent level" instead of asking your audience to read the standard errors and navigate their way through every element of your slide. Also, remember to unify your presentation color aesthetic by using colors from your presentation color palette, not the defaults from your software.

While this kind of pared-down table is serviceable, moving to a visual presentation of the data works even better. Thinking visually and creating content that taps into the strengths of our eyes and brains will help your audience effortlessly process the numbers and understand your conclusions. It may even allow you to add back some of the detail pared out of the table initially (such as standard errors or other variables) to make it more workable for the audience.

In the following example, the first slide shows the estimates for each variable across the four models, while the second slide adds error bars to denote statistical significance (alternatively, you could add asterisks above the bars). Depending on how much detail you want to cover with these results, you could then apply the layering technique to the slide and show the four estimates for the first model, then the estimates for the second model, and so on.

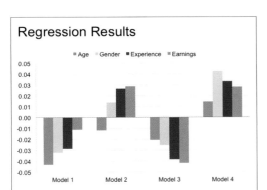
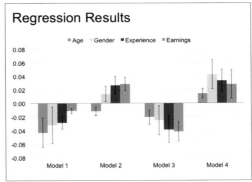

Try to visualize your data when possible.

INSERTING GRAPHS

So what about actually creating and importing graphs into your presentation? Most researchers have a preferred program for data visualizations, be it a standard desktop program like Excel, a design tool like Adobe Illustrator, or programming languages like R and Stata. Sometimes these tools will be combined, with statistical analysis conducted in programs like SPSS or SAS, and the final graphs created and styled in Excel. Some researchers create their graphs directly in their presentation software while developing their slides.

Any of these approaches can be successful, though each presents slightly different challenges when it comes to creating your presentation. Creating an image in one tool and importing it into your slide software may require testing the different image file formats, the size, and how the colors and fonts will appear when projected. You may also need to go back and forth between different programs as you edit and iterate.

If you choose to create graphs directly in your slide presentation tool (PowerPoint or otherwise), you should end up with high-resolution graphs. However, it will also make the data available (potentially problematic) to anyone who has the file. Another potential downside is that your presentation tool may not have the same data visualization capabilities as a chart-building tool, so it may not be able to give you exactly what you want.

Whether you create your graphs in another tool and paste them into your slide software, or you make them directly in the slide tool itself, you may need to align and arrange the

INSERTING EXCEL CHARTS IN POWERPOINT

There are two primary ways to paste Excel graphs into PowerPoint—as images or as objects. If you insert your Excel charts as images, you may find that they appear blurry or distorted. To avoid this, I use the *Enhanced MetaFile (EMF)* format (on Windows) or the *PDF* format (on Macs), which usually generate high quality images on my slides. I have also learned to make the graphs in Excel as large as the slide. That way, when I paste them into PowerPoint, I don't have to resize or stretch them, which can lower the resolution (quality) of the image.

You can also copy a graph in Excel and paste it into PowerPoint, where it will appear as an Object. The advantages are that the resolution remains intact, the chart will look sharp on the slide, and you can format individual elements, such as lines, bars, or data markers (you can then also animate those elements using PowerPoint's *Animation* tools). The disadvantage of this approach is that anyone you send the file to may be able to see and edit your graphs and data—advantageous if you are collaborating with others on a presentation, but problematic if you have proprietary or restricted data you do not want others to access. This strategy can also backfire if you don't save the raw Excel file or if you move the Excel or PowerPoint file to a different location or computer. PowerPoint will try to look for the original file and if it can't find it, you may end up with a blank graph. So if you use this approach, be sure to keep your files together, especially if you need to transfer them to another computer.

graphs across the different slides. For example, if you layer a set of graphs, it's crucial that the axes, titles, and labels all stay in the same position so that the only thing that moves from one slide to the next is the plotted data. To do so, make sure the graphs are the same size and positioned in the same place on each slide. Alternatively, once you have positioned one of your graphs exactly where you want it, you can copy and paste it to another slide to help you position the new graph. Arrange the new graph to be consistent with the original one, and then delete it.

For very simple charts, you may not need to use a graphing tool. One approach I've taken in cases where I need a simple bar or column chart is to just use shapes. For example, to create a column chart with three columns—2 percent, 3 percent, and 6 percent—you can draw three columns of different lengths (2 inches, 3 inches, and 6 inches), and then scale all three down simultaneously to fit on the slide.

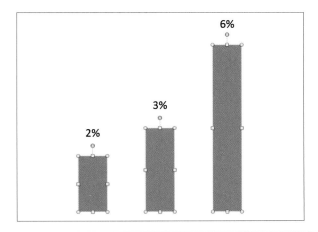

Simple charts can sometimes be drawn and then aligned.

▶   ▶   ▶   ▶   ▶

While data visualizations may be the core image type for most researchers, you can also use photographs, icons, and illustrations to help convey your content. These kinds of images can be useful devices for adding purposeful designs, tying different slide or presentation elements together, encouraging your audience to focus on your slides, and helping your audience to better remember your message. In the next chapter, I will show what constitutes effective kinds of images, how to find and download them, and how to insert and edit them into your presentation file.

THREE THINGS TO REMEMBER ABOUT
THE DATA VISUALIZATION SLIDE

1. **Visualize.** Tap into the brain's preattentive visual processing by using elements such as color, lines, shapes, and markings to highlight and show your data.
2. **Unify.** Link your text and your visuals; for example, integrate your legends directly into your graphs.
3. **Focus.** Help your audience better see the data by minimizing or eliminating nonessential elements including gridlines, tick marks, and data labels.

THE IMAGE SLIDE

In this chapter, I move from visuals that explicitly communicate information (such as graphs and tables), to ones that visually support the speaker by framing or giving context to the presentation. Some presenters avoid these kinds of supporting images, preferring to "stick with the facts" and focus on text and data. However, images serve an important function in presentations, because the audience will learn and remember more when your spoken word is combined with an image (this is the "Picture Superiority Effect" that guides the *visualize* principle, as discussed in the Introduction). In a large set of experiments conducted in the 1980s, psychologist Alan Paivio found that an audience is twice as likely to recall a topic if it includes an image. More recently, in a series of experiments in which audiences were shown different presentation styles of the same content, psychologist Joanna Garner and her colleagues showed that audiences had better comprehension from presentations that were more visual. In addition, the body of research by Richard Mayer and colleagues on different learning styles has also demonstrated the value of using images and pairing them with text. It is important to remember that your images should support your content and not be included merely for decorative purposes.

This section of the book is not about convincing you to find beautiful images just to make your slides look pretty. Instead, it is intended to encourage you to find and include images that support your spoken message. Images can also help make your content elicit an emotional response from your audience. Even with a highly sophisticated or technical group, appealing to your audience's emotions can engage them in ways that text and numbers cannot. Emotions (or *affect*, as defined in psychology) can influence different cognitive processes like memory, creativity, and attention. Activating your audience's emotions induces attachment, helping them connect with and remember you and your content.

MAKE YOUR IMAGES FULL-SCREEN

In general, take advantage of your entire slide space instead of just using the default image size. Maximizing the image so that it fills the entire slide will not only make it easier for the audience to see, but it will also reduce unnecessary blank space. The same strategy applies to multiple images—arrange and unify them with the text to fill the full space, instead of randomly placing them on the slide. This will minimize the amount of mental work your audience has to do trying to figure out what's on the slide, and will allow them to concentrate on your argument and message.

Avoid images that are too small, are of poor quality, have watermarks, or are stretched in weird ways. Even if your audience is not composed of designers, they can still recognize bad or cliché images, and may end up distracted, chuckling at the picture of some executive jumping on the beach rather than listening to you talk. With so many great resources for high-quality, relevant images—many of them free—bad images are universally unacceptable.

Consider a presentation on the challenges facing young girls in developing countries. The basic slide many researchers would create might look something like this, full of

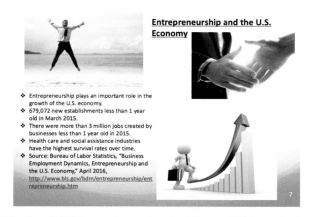

Avoid bad or cliché stock images.

Challenges for Girls' Education in Developing Countries

- 80 countries where progress has stalled
  - These countries are not meeting the UN Millennium Development Goals.
  - An additional 30 countries have successfully enrolled children in primary and secondary education, but provide low-quality learning
- Early marriage and teen pregnancy
  - 1 in 3 girls in low- and middle-income countries are married before the age of 18;
  - 1 in 9 are married before age 15
- School-related violence
  - Ranges from bullying and exploitation to kidnapping and bombing.

The typical text slide (Content based on King and Winthrop, 2015)

text, inconsistent punctuation, bullet points and sub-bullet points, all in the default Calibri font.

Following the strategies from chapter 4, you can start by reducing a good portion of the text, which will automatically open up more space on the slide. With the quantity of text reduced, you now have room for an image that can help the audience visualize the content and make it personal for them. You are more likely to remember the slide on the right than the slide on the left because I've added a content-relevant image. You'll also notice that I've removed the actual bullet points. The bullets separate portions of text, but by reducing the amount of text on the slide, you can let the white space act as the separator.

Challenges for Girls' Education in Developing Countries

- 80 countries where progress has stalled
- Early marriage and teen pregnancy
- School-related violence

Challenges for Girls' Education in Developing Countries

80 countries where progress has stalled

Early marriage and teen pregnancy

School-related violence

Reducing text opens up space on the slide, which can be used to add a content-relevant image

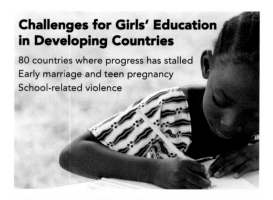 

Make the image full-screen and increase the text size

We can make this image larger, fill the slide, and move the text to the lighter parts of the image. As we did for text slides, consider the person at the back of the room and utilize all of the available slide space.

If you have text that overlaps the active or darker parts of an image, or if the image doesn't have sufficient blank or light space, then you can use a transparent shape to help offset the text to let it stand out. When you're working with a more crowded image, you can choose a color from the picture itself for the background of the text box, and increase

Eliminate the bullet point text altogether and let the image fill the slide

its transparency to enable you to still see the full picture (you may need to use the *Arrange* menu in PowerPoint to organize the different objects on your slide, depending on what order you've added them).

You could also eliminate all of the text and leave only the title. Again, we are designing for the back row, using an active, Twitter-like title, and using an image that fills the screen.

There may be times when you want to use multiple images on a single slide. In such cases, still try to use the entire slide space. Notice the difference just a slight rearrangement and resizing makes for the four images about nutrition programs. With the full slide space used and the text integrated with the images, you achieve a more unified, harmonious look that reduces the amount of visual navigation your audience has to do. To mimic this kind of layout, you can resize the images and align them together (you can do this in PowerPoint using the *Align* menu). You can then add lines to separate the images either by adding a border to each photo or by simply drawing lines on the slide.

As you pair text with images, play with the positioning to find a layout that best unifies both elements. For instance, if you want to pair a quote from author Seth Godin with a photograph of him, your first instinct may be to put the photograph in the center, with the quote off to the side, as on the next page. While this arrangement does succeed in putting a great deal of emphasis on the image, the content (his quote) is given less prominence. Also, the text is somewhat cramped so that everything fits (I've used a 32 pt font size).

Unify images by arranging them so they fill the slide space (Photos, clockwise from top-right: Anda Abrosini, Lotte Löhr, Harshal Hirve, and Irina Blok, Unsplash.com)

One way to fix this would be to move Godin to the right, so that you can increase the size of the quote and use the full space of the slide. This is a significant improvement—the text is bigger with a 40+ pt font size (again, you're designing for the back of the room), and the content now has as much prominence as the image.

Notice, however, how Godin's eyes look away from the text. Whenever you pair an image of a person with text, try to unify the two elements by situating the image so that it leads

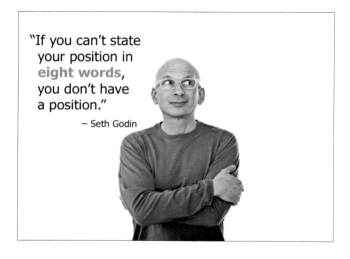

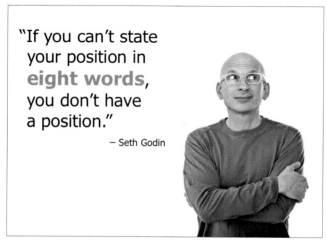

Moving the image to one side opens space for larger text (Photo: Brian Bloom)

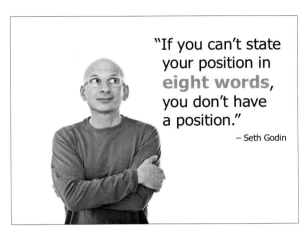

Unify the image and the text by having the subject look at the text.
More generally, align your text with the shape of your images.

REMOVING IMAGE BACKGROUND

The original image in the Seth Godin example came with a white background. What happens if you're presenting in a dark room and aren't using a white background? You can remove the background of the photo in many presentation programs like Power-Point (by using the *Remove Background* tool) and Keynote (by using the *Instant Alpha* tool). Tools like Beamer do not include the same functionality, but you could edit the image in PowerPoint, save it, and then insert it into your Beamer presentation. Also in this example, I used PowerPoint's *Align* tool to place the image at the bottom of the slide to avoid having it look as if he is floating in space.

 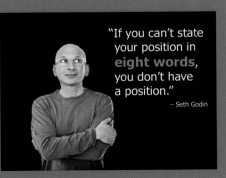

your audience's eye *toward* the text. If you move the photo to left side of the slide and the text to the right, your audience will naturally follow Godin's eyes to his quote.

With this layout, you connect a face to a quote, but still give the content—the quote—a place of distinction on the slide. More generally, you can unify your images (especially active images like a person walking or a plane flying) and text by aligning the text with a shape in the image. As a simple example, recall the pyramid images from chapter 1 and how the text was aligned along the diagonal of the shape. By taking a little time to play around with image and text placement, you can make sure your images feel unified with the text and engage, rather than distract, your audience.

Keeping some of these general guidelines in mind, I'll now turn to finding, downloading, inserting, and formatting images and videos.

FINDING GOOD IMAGES

The presentation worksheet in chapter 1 has a space for you to sketch and list ideas for images. Here's where specificity in this section becomes useful. As soon as you search the Internet for "climate change" or "income distribution" or "international finance," you undoubtedly find generic stock images that relate to your content in only a peripheral way. Having a concrete sense of the actual image you're looking for will lead to better results. Instead, try "coastal damages from Hurricane Sandy" or "homelessness in Washington, DC" or "Greek bank runs." Think carefully about what you want the image to say, and how you want it to look. Avoid the posed, cliché, or unnatural images, and bypass sight gags or sarcasm, unless it fits in with your content and tone.

As you start your search, you can use the composition guideline known as the "Rule of Thirds" to direct your selection of images. According to the rule of thirds, images appear more interesting, dynamic, and engaging if the subject is not placed directly in the center. As the name suggests, imagine dividing your image or slide into nine parts by sectioning it into thirds horizontally and vertically. Photographer David Peterson suggests the rule of thirds works because when the subject of the image is placed in the center it appears static; your eyes are drawn directly to it with nowhere to go. However, when the subject is placed closer to the edges, it forces your eyes to follow it and encourages the viewer to look at the image longer. In this way the image becomes more interactive. Recall the Seth Godin slide: when he's moved from the middle to the left, the slide appears more active and has sufficient space for larger, headline text.

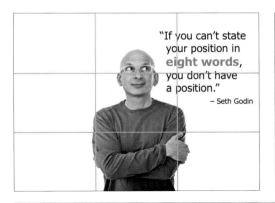 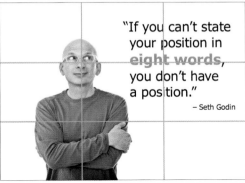

Use the Rule of Thirds to make images more active and unify slide objects.

In his e-book *Slides Made Simple,* Adam Noar has a few other good suggestions for identifying images that will work as the full background for the slide. First, use images with significant whitespace (the empty space between objects) so that you can add text or other content. Next, photos with blurred areas can give you additional space to include other slide objects without covering up important areas of the image. Last, photos in which colors slowly fade (gradients) from one color to another can allow for the seamless placing of text and other objects.

These guidelines aren't hard and fast. You may find that a busy or dense photograph is exactly what you need to best communicate your argument, and you can present it alongside text (possibly by using a transparent text box as I did earlier) or alone on a slide without any text or other objects. Keep in mind your audience is going to try to decipher everything you put on the screen, and the more complex the image and the more random its placement, the less focused they will be.

PHOTO RESOURCES

So where do you find suitable photos—aside from just typing keywords into Google and seeing what comes up? For me, a good photo website offers a large, high-quality selection and an easy-to-use search tool. Below are some suggestions of both free and paid resources. These resources are always changing and new tools and sites are constantly emerging. I maintain a current list on the book's website.

ISTOCKPHOTO, SHUTTERSTOCK, AND CORBIS IMAGES, TO START. These are just three of the many for-pay photo sites available on the Web, each of which has different subscription and purchase options. Be aware that some of these sites have different licensing agreements for different uses (e.g., use in a book versus use in a lecture for your undergraduate course).

FLICKR CREATIVE COMMONS. This is a photo-posting and sharing site with millions of users around the world. By default, many of these photos are available for free and for use through the Creative Commons licensing (more in a later section on what this licensing means).

COMPFIGHT. Compfight taps into the same Flickr library, but I think it has a better display and search tool. You can filter search results by different tags or licenses, either Creative Commons or Commercial. Search results yield pages of thumbnail images you can see immediately with a selection of images near the top that are not from Flickr but from commercial photography sites.

FREE IMAGES. This site contains nearly half-a-million free images with pretty broad licensing. You can use the images in multiple platforms (e.g., printed and digital) for both commercial and noncommercial use. Most images do not require attribution, though you should check their licensing documentation before ultimately using any of the images you find here.

PEXELS. Images you find on Pexels can be used for free and without attribution for both personal and commercial use, making it a terrific resource if you don't have a budget for purchasing photos. Other good websites that provide completely free images (some of which Pexels searches) are Pixabay, Unsplash, Gratisography, and Little Visuals.

WIKIMEDIA COMMONS. Using the same philosophy as Wikipedia, Wikimedia Commons acts as an image repository for public domain and freely-licensed media content, including images, sound, and video, but you will still need to check individual licenses for each piece.

You'll notice that Google Images is missing from this list. I don't recommend using images from Google for two primary reasons: First, most images are sized for use on the Internet and the image resolution is not always high enough for presentations, especially with higher-resolution high-definition screens and projectors. Second, usage permissions on Google images are not always accurate because images can appear on different websites, not all of which respect copyright rules. You should always be sure you are legally allowed to use an image (more on this below).

ICON RESOURCES

As with photographs, icons can be used to make you and your slides more engaging and memorable. Similar to color and font, icons can be used throughout your presentation to help connect and unify different segments of your discussion. As an alternative approach to the previous Girls' Education slide example, instead of removing the bullet points and inserting a large image, you could combine text, shapes, and icons to communicate your point. Notice how the icons give you a clear, visual clue to the topic. The icons could then be repeated on subsequent slides to help the audience organize the talk in their minds. Another option is to layer the headline and the three points as separate slides, which would allow you to make each icon larger; for example, placing a larger version of the map on its own slide where you could highlight the 80 countries.

As with photo sites, there are lots of options available (more are listed on the book's website):

FLAT ICON. A large database of simple icons, the vast majority of which are free to use with no attribution. Many are provided as multiple icons in a single image, so you will need to make good use of your slide software's cropping tools.

ICONMNSTR. This site hosts more than 3,000 icons, all free for use and with no attribution required. Iconmnstr contains high-quality icons, but there are fewer options to choose from.

NOUN PROJECT. This is an online community of designers who contribute their own icons to the library. There are different download and purchasing options available. You can download icons for free as long as you attribute the designer, or you can purchase icons for under $5.

Icons can be useful visual objects to help communicate content.

CUSTOM IMAGES

If you have the budget and inclination, you can also purchase custom-made images and icons. There is no shortage of capable, creative people willing to help you create great, effective icons and images. A few resources you might use include 99 designs, Bēhance, Dribbble, Fiverr, and Upwork. These and others are websites that enable you to connect with people with multiple skills, ranging from Web and graphic designers to illustrators, artists, coders, developers, typographers, and others. Once you sign up, you can browse individual portfolios searchable by skill, type of work, and location, among others.

COPYRIGHTS AND ATTRIBUTION

Because it's so easy to find and download images from the Internet, many presenters often do so without thinking about who created them or who they belong to. As a result, they often fail to ensure they have obtained the proper permissions to use these images in their presentations. This may appear to be a small thing, but consider how carefully we are to cite other people's research in our work. As presenters, we should extend the same courtesy to creators of visual content. Someone has created the image you just downloaded from the Internet, and you may need permission to use it.

The advantage of using a for-profit photo website like those listed above (and on the book's website) is that they include information about copyrights and permissions with the photo itself. If you purchase an image from a site like iStockPhoto or Shutterstock, you typically have the right to use it how you see fit without any further attribution (be sure to check the permissions from the source website to confirm). Websites like Compfight, which feature many images for use without charge, will specify how you should attribute the image when you use it. On such sites, permissions and attribution requirements will generally be communicated through Creative Commons licensing, allowing others to use their work freely and easily.

Creative Commons (CC) licenses can be applied to any creative product, such as videos, graphics, or photos. There are six licenses available that stipulate what you can and cannot do with the licensed work. For example, the "Attribution (CC BY)" license (the "BY" stands for attribution) allows you to do whatever you like with a creative product (including using it for commercial purposes) as long as you give appropriate credit to the creator. By comparison, the "Attribution-NonCommercial-NoDerivs (CC BY-NC-ND)" license is the most restrictive of the six licenses. It requires you to credit the work ("BY"), use it in noncommercial projects only ("NC"), and make no changes (derivatives) to it ("ND"). All CC licenses are made in perpetuity, even if the content creator removes the image from the original site. You can find full descriptions of each type of license on the CC website.

If the licensing on an image isn't clear or prohibits the use you had in mind, you can always request permission by simply asking the creator. I once found a great photo on Compfight, but the photographer had restricted its copyright use. I requested permission to use the image via email, which he gladly granted.

Also, be careful about using images in multiple mediums. Having permission to use an image in your PowerPoint presentation doesn't necessarily give you permission to use it on your website, in a journal article, or in a book (which can move you from "noncommercial" to "commercial" use). Restrictions can even encompass conferences that would like to post your slides on their website. Therefore, you may want to stick with images having licenses that allow for both commercial and noncommercial use, or make a broader request to the creator or website so that you can include the image in different products.

Adding an attribution to an image in your slides is quite simple: At the bottom of your slide, include something like "*Photo: Jon Schwabish*" or "*Photo Credit: Jon Schwabish.*" You may also want to include the source of the image: "*Photo Credit: Flickr/Jon Schwabish.*" You can put the attribution text box anywhere on your slide, but I usually prefer to put it in the lower-right corner of the slide, in 12- or 14-point italicized font. For more complicated attributions—for example, citing an entire publication—you can include additional information in the "endnote" slide mentioned in the previous chapter.

GET LARGER IMAGES

How your images ultimately appear on the screen will depend on the quality of the image and your hardware (more on the latter below). Images are made of pixels, the smallest single component of a digital image (you may have heard the phrase "dot per inch" (dpi) or "pixels per inch" (ppi); these terms reflect the density of dots or pixels on the page or screen). The more pixels used in an image, the higher the resolution and the closer the image resembles the original. If you make an image smaller, you increase the dots per inch (the dots get tighter and tighter). Hence, doing so should not distort the image. However, if you make an image larger, you decrease the dots per inch (lessening the density of the dots), which may result in a blurry or distorted image.

Stretching your images too much may generate blurs or distortions

Therefore, I recommend you download the largest image available. The image on the left was originally 1.67″ wide × 1.11″ tall when inserted into PowerPoint. It needed to stretch quite a bit to fit the slide space (I've zoomed in on the girl's shoulder). By comparison, the larger version of the image, shown here on the right, was 6.63″ × 10″ when inserted into PowerPoint. Therefore, it stretched just slightly to fit the 7.5″ × 10″ slide (more on slide dimensions in the next chapter). If you look closely, you can see the difference in the quality between the two images.

In most cases, irrespective of your image size and pixels count, the quality of the image on the screen will ultimately be determined by the quality of your projector. Standard projectors might show 800 pixels wide by 600 pixels tall while newer, high-resolution definitions might show 4,000 pixels by 2,000 pixels. Testing your presentation on the projector you will use is the best way to know how your images will look. If you don't have that luxury, try to find images with the largest size and highest quality (even though they'll likely require more computer memory).

SAVING AND INSERTING IMAGES

Now that you have identified an image, the next step is to get it off the Internet, onto your computer, and into your presentation. Let's return to the image of the young girl in the Girls' Education slide. I purchased three different sizes of this image from Shutterstock, and saved them to my computer in the same folder that holds the presentation file.

EDITING IMAGES IN POWERPOINT

Most presentation tools have fairly decent image-editing tools. For example, in Power-Point you can remove parts of an image by using the *Crop* tool. PowerPoint's *Crop* tool only edits images vertically and horizontally. If you want to remove other parts of an image, consider hiding them by placing shapes on top of the image (in this image of the U.S., I've "cropped" Hawaii and Alaska by placing rectangles on top of them and I will then change the color to match the white background).

You can also change the transparency of your images directly by using the editing tools or by adding a transparent shape on top of the image. If you're concerned about the size of your presentation file, you can use PowerPoint's *Compress* option to reduce the file size and remove the unused parts of the images you have cropped. (Note: once you compress a cropped image, you can't recover those pieces of the image later should you want to edit it again). PowerPoint does some default compressing automatically, which is why your images may degrade over time as you edit and reuse your presentation file.

As you start downloading images, it's worth spending some time considering how you want to organize your image library. Depending on the website, the file may have been named something obscure like "8142413786_fbd8d37852_h.jpg," which isn't very helpful when you are searching your files for the image you downloaded last week. It also makes it difficult to keep track of the image attribution.

My primary method for keeping my images organized is to create separate folders on my computer for each presentation. Within each folder, I create an "Images" folder in which all of the original images are placed. When I insert them into my slide deck, I include the source and attribution information on the slide or in the Notes pane. Then, if I want to use the image again, I have the raw image and the slide already created, which contains the original URL. Of course, there are many other methods you can use, especially if you have images that are not presentation specific:

▸ Rename the actual file name with the source website, author, and possibly a keyword. This strategy will allow you to hold onto the different attributions of the image, but it will create long file names and may clutter your folder view.

▸ Insert all of your images into a single presentation to serve as your image library. In this file, record the source location, attribution details, and other information on the slide or in the Notes pane. Over time, this will likely generate a large file, which may be hard to maintain, so you may need to create several of these "library" presentation files. I usually create these library files for each presentation separately, which I can then move around if I am going to reuse the image in a different presentation.

▸ Save all of your images in a single folder and record the relevant information (file name, title, and source) in a spreadsheet. In this way, you can identify the images using their original file names, but also have an accounting of the source information you may need later on.

▸ There are a variety of online services like Pinterest and Evernote that are built to organize images and other content. For example, Pinterest allows you to essentially create a visual bookmark of the image linked to the original source.

USING VIDEO

Videos can help change the pace of your presentation and naturally engage your audience. However, as with all other material, they should always be used to help support your message and content, and not just because you found a cool video you want to share.

Presentation author Garr Reynolds recommends keeping video clips to under 30 seconds. With longer clips, he argues, you may begin to lose your audience. I find the length of the video is not as important as the quality of the content. In some presentations, I show a two-and-a-half minute clip from Hans Rosling's famous TED Talk, *The best stats you've ever seen*. It's clever, funny, and interesting. My audience seems just as entertained as the original TED audience.

Seamlessly transitioning from a slide to a video is easy, if you set it up the right way. If possible, try to avoid switching between your presentation software and the video software or Internet browser. This is especially true when it comes to streaming video from a website, which will require a reliable Internet connection. Instead, download the video onto your computer and insert it into your presentation (in PowerPoint, you can easily add video to your slides by using the *Insert* menu). Once your video is safely on your slide, you can resize it, rotate it, and stretch it. Consistent with my recommendation that images should take up the entire slide space, I also ensure my videos play on a full-screen (video-sizing options are available in the *Format Movie* menu in PowerPoint). Note that adding videos to your presentation will significantly increase the file size. PowerPoint does give you the option of compressing your videos into different levels of quality (select *File* and then *Info*), but you should double-check the quality of the video after compression.

Hans Rosling, *The best stats you've ever seen*, TED Talk, February 2006, used with permission

Also, having the video file on your machine will allow you to edit it to the specific clip you intend to use. There are a variety of paid and free tools you can use to download videos to your computer. Basic video-editing tools are available on both Windows (Windows Movie Maker) and Mac OS (QuickTime and iMovie) computers, and they will enable you to trim videos to the desired length.

I also recommend you keep your videos in the same folder as your presentation. PowerPoint, in particular, will look for the raw video file and if you move it from the original location, you may not be able to play it. Similarly, if you use a program like Beamer, your code will point to the original file location, so moving the file without updating the code will be problematic. By keeping everything together, if you experience difficulties with your computer or you need to share the presentation with someone else, everything can be easily packaged together.

▶ ▶ ▶ ▶ ▶

Hopefully, you can now see the power of images in presentations. We are more likely to remember, recognize, and connect with content when it is anchored with a visual. As a researcher, you can easily insert images into your slides—be they photographs, illustrations, or icons—to help your audience better grasp and remember your message. As with text and graphs, maximize your use of the slide area by obtaining large images and making them full-screen. You can pair simple, headline-like text with those images to help support what you say and focus your audience's attention on the specific point or argument.

THREE THINGS TO REMEMBER ABOUT THE IMAGE SLIDE

1. **Visualize.** Use large, high-quality (high-resolution) images that fill the entire slide space.
2. **Unify.** Be consistent in your use of images across your presentation. If you're going to use black-and-white photographs for the first ten slides, don't depart from that aesthetic for slide eleven.
3. **Focus.** Link text and images so that they draw the audience's attention to the important parts of your slide.

THE SCAFFOLDING SLIDES

I f you've followed the strategies presented so far, you now have a presentation that features less text, clean data visualizations designed to focus audience attention, and images intended to support your points and engage your viewers. With all of this in place, there is one final family of slides—what I call scaffolding slides—that will ensure your audience is able to follow your argument and understand your message.

The purpose of scaffolding slides is to guide and focus your audience's attention as you transition from one section to another, and to drive home important points. They act as scaffolding because they don't carry the message or content themselves, but rather support the delivery of this information. Scaffolding slides are a family of different slide types, which include the *title* and *agenda* slides for introducing your presentation, *header* slides to divide your presentation into sections, *breaker* slides that redirect attention back to you, and *ending* slides for concluding your presentation.

TITLE SLIDES

I would hazard a guess that 99 percent of the scholarly presentations you've seen lead with a slide that includes the title of the presentation, the author's name and affiliation, and some contact information. You and your fellow audience members spend a good deal of time looking at this slide as you wait for the presentation to begin. Yet usually it's nondescript,

Creating a better title slide that is more visual and engaging
(Photo: Ryan McGuire, Gratisography.com)

suggesting nothing of content, and failing to tap into the visual parts of your brain. This is clearly a wasted opportunity. Your first slide can help set the tone, so use it to emphasize that you intend to deliver a substantive, engaging, and enjoyable presentation where they will undoubtedly take away valuable content.

First, think about what you can eliminate to reduce clutter and increase focus on the critical information. Do you need to list your full title, presentation date, email address, mailing address, and phone number? (And really, do you *want* people calling you?) Maybe your email is the only contact detail actually required. Once you've decided what to remove, think about what you might add. Are there complementary images that will reinforce your content? Finally, make sure you unify all the elements on the slide, with the same font and colors used in the presentation. To see the difference this can make, consider the following: Which slide above signals that the presenter has given careful thought to their slides? Which is most considerate of the needs of the audience? Finally, which slide is more likely to be memorable and useful to the audience?

AGENDA SLIDES

The more prepared your audience is for how you are going to deliver your message, the better they will follow along. Agenda slides can be very helpful in providing this roadmap, but not every agenda slide does this effectively. Often such slides seem to be more for the

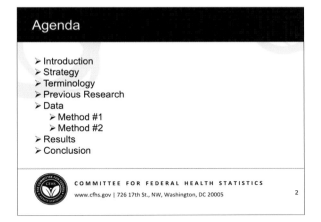

The typical agenda slide

speaker, reminding her what she's going to say, than for the audience—in which case, it is better not to include it at all. Instead, simply say it—remember, not everything you say needs to go on a slide. The agenda slide shown above lists everything the presenter is going to do, but provides little value for the audience. It gives the audience no indication of the importance of the rest of the presentation, how much time will be spent on each section, or what they will learn.

The other option is to use an alternative to the classic agenda slide, such as a timeline, as on the next page. Instead of using the standard bullet-point, text-driven approach, the timeline-agenda slide helps set the audience's expectations for the structure of the presentation and thus adds context. In this example, I've deleted some of the repetitious bullets and organized the remaining bullets in a timeline using the same text (I built this timeline directly in PowerPoint using rectangles sized proportionally to the expected amount of time spent on each section). You could also layer this slide one step at a time, which would allow the presenter to say more about each section, maybe adding a statement about *why* it's important. But consider whether it's worth spending this additional time talking about what you plan to talk about. Maybe just getting directly into your content would be more valuable.

This kind of timeline-style slide can be particularly helpful if you have a full day of separate presentations or exercises with scheduled breaks. In this case, your audience will appreciate knowing you've anticipated their needs for breaks, snacks, and lunch. They can then set their own expectations for the longer day.

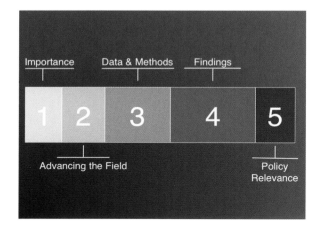

A timeline-agenda slide (after Reynolds, 2008)

Another alternative to the classic agenda slide is to use icons, and to configure the slide in a way that helps communicate the relationship between different sections of your presentation. This will give your audience a big-picture idea of what's to come and provide a visual cue for each topic, which can be repeated over the course of the presentation. Again, I eliminated some of the bullet points and replaced the remaining ones with more memorable icons.

Agenda slide that replaces bullets with icons

HEADER SLIDES

If you followed the presentation worksheet in chapter 1, your presentation should already be broken up into several sections. As you move through your presentation, you can give your audience guideposts as sections begin and end, so they can follow your argument. These header slides, as I call them, help your audience get a sense of where you are and where you're headed by explicitly directing their attention as you move from one section to the next.

Header slides typically include the section title and maybe a relevant image or icon (depending on your preference). You could even just use a large number, perhaps paired with

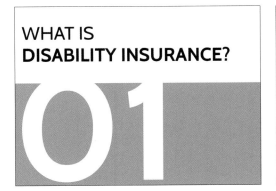

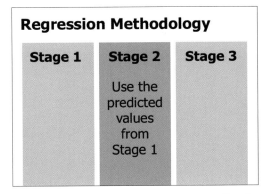

Examples of header slides (Top-right: Kevin Dooley)

a shape or image. These slides are not difficult to construct and will be very useful for your audience, who, ideally, are trying to absorb and organize the information internally as you present it. Samples of other header slide examples are provided on the book's website, which you can download and edit for your own use.

You don't need to linger on these transition slides. For example, following your discussion of the previous literature, you may simply show your "Regression Methodology" header slide and then say, "Now that I've given you a sense of what others have done in this field, I'm going to tell you about the data I used and how I implemented it in my model." Another advantage of the header slide is that you can do away with the title of subsequent slides. For example, the phrase "Regression Methodology" does not need to be repeated at the top of the next set of slides showing the estimation steps. Doing so frees up space to add content or, better yet, to make the content larger.

There are other strategies you can use to transition from one section to another. You could play a short video, tell a story, conduct an interactive exercise with the audience, or take a break for questions. Anything that signals to your audience that you are moving from one section to the next—say, from "Data" to "Results"—will help keep them focused on your path through your content. Research from the 1970s (and supported by more recent research described in Ruth Clark and Richard Mayer's book on instruction, and by *Brain Rules'* author John Medina) suggests that people's attention usually starts to decline about 10 minutes after the beginning of a lecture or presentation. Medina uses "hooks" to reengage his audience every 10 minutes; such hooks are foremost "very relevant to the provided content" (121) and might be unusual case histories, anecdotes, or other stories. These hooks break the pace of the presentation and pull people back to the content and message. By clearly transitioning from one section of your presentation to another, your audience will be better able to follow you.

BREAKER SLIDES

I rarely see breaker slides used in presentations, but they can be extremely effective in guiding audience focus. Breaker slides are also a breeze to create because they have nothing on them. That's right, breaker slides are completely blank.

What's the purpose of a blank slide in the middle of a presentation? Imagine you've shown slide after slide with text and graphs and tables, while talking the entire time. Your

Breaker slides

audience may be a little worn out, perhaps even a bit bored. They're trying to process a lot at once, and may have transitioned into auto-pilot—looking at your slides and listening to you talk without really taking anything in. Cue the breaker slide. It not only snaps audience members back to attention—"Huh? Why am I looking at a blank screen?"—but it also gives them a moment to rest their brains (once they realize its intention). More importantly, it encourages them to turn their focus back to you because there's nothing on the screen to draw their attention.

You can purposefully insert a separate, blank slide directly into your slide deck, or in PowerPoint's slideshow mode, you can hit the "W" key to get a white screen or the "B" key to get a black screen (some slide clickers have a built-in breaker slide key). Hitting the key again will bring you back to your presentation.

ENDING SLIDES

The presentation is coming to an end. The speaker had you hooked right from the beginning with a powerful opening story that helped drive the narrative. Throughout, he clearly and concisely described his data and methodology. As he nears the end with ample time left over, he thanks the audience for their attention, and projects his last slide, which shows a single word: "Questions?"

These final "Thank You!" and "Questions?" slides are wasted opportunities that don't leave your audience with your final, concluding statements. Instead, they signal an end to

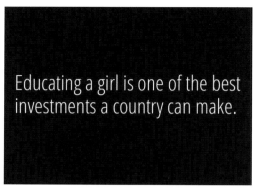

Replace ending slides that don't have content with an active, concluding statement.

the presentation. So while some audience members may have questions, others will start packing up their belongings. Remember, you don't need to put everything you say on the screen: You can simply say "Thank you for having me" or "What questions do you have?" and save the slide space for something more powerful.

You've already constructed a concise, active headline from the worksheet in chapter 1, so use it here. Place that sentence or phrase on the screen or pair it with an image. You want people to leave the room—especially those who have engaged you with questions and discussions—with your concluding statements utmost in their minds. If you are in a smaller group setting with a list of things you and your audience want to accomplish after your talk, a "Talking Points" or "To Do" list might be appropriate. Also, your final slide could show your email, Twitter handle, or other contact information.

TAKING A DIFFERENT VIEW OF YOUR PRESENTATION

As you work through your presentation, you may find yourself becoming a bit lost in the collection of text, images, graphs, and tables. If you're using PowerPoint, you can easily get a bird's eye view of your presentation using the *Slide Sorter* view (found in the *View* menu). Similarly, in Keynote you can use the *Light Table* view. In these views, your slides are arranged as thumbnail images. This perspective can be useful when you want to review how sections of your presentation hang together, if you are rearranging a presentation, or if you are combining pieces from different presentations. These views can also be beneficial for checking whether you have a consistent look across your entire talk. Many presentation software programs help you to organize your slides by grouping them. In PowerPoint, you can create "Sections," which will place multiple slides into groups. In Keynote, you can indent a group of slides to make them subordinate to another slide. This organizational technique can be especially useful if you have a number of slides, enabling you to easily see and organize the different parts of your talk.

▶ ▶ ▶ ▶ ▶

At this point, we move from building the presentation to giving the presentation. You have thoughtfully and strategically designed and constructed your presentation. Using the Presentation Worksheet in chapter 1, you've thought about how to deliver the content verbally and know not to simply move your written report into slides. Using the design principles covered in chapters 2 and 3, you've decided on a consistent color palette across your slides and selected a font (or two). Your slides now have large text, headline titles, and minimal (if any) bullets (chapter 4), and your graphs consider how someone in your audience will view them differently from someone who is reading your report at their desk (chapter 5). In addition, throughout, you've made your presentation more visual with better colors, fonts, graphs, and images. Now that you have created an effective slide deck, it's time to go out and deliver your content. The next section covers actually giving the presentation and the tools you might need to accompany you.

THREE THINGS TO REMEMBER ABOUT SCAFFOLDING SLIDES

1. **Visualize.** Large visuals—possibly simple text—can act as simple markers to break or introduce sections in your presentation.
2. **Unify.** Use similar colors, fonts, images, and icons to help guide your audience through your presentation.
3. **Focus.** Scaffolding slides help you guide and focus your audience's attention as you transition from one section to another.

PART THREE

GIVING YOUR PRESENTATION

PRESENTING

Y ou've made it this far. You've developed your content, constructed an outline, crafted your opening and closing statements, and chosen the overall look of the presentation. You've created slides that are light on text and heavy on data visualizations and images, and that will engage your audience with a message they will (hopefully) be persuaded by and act upon. Now that you've put in all this work, it's time to actually give your presentation.

Aside from your content and slides, your presence in front of your audience will help shape how they react to your message. You may have spent countless hours developing your analysis and building your slides, but at the end of the day, presentations are about standing before a group of people and communicating your ideas. In this chapter, I'll focus on strategies for preparing for and delivering your presentation. In the next chapter, I'll look at some of the technical details to keep in mind before, during, and after.

PREPARING FOR YOUR PRESENTATION

One of the most important things you can do to give a great presentation is to practice. And practice. And practice some more. You can practice your 15-minute conference presentation four times in an hour and that's probably four more times than anyone else at the conference—and it will show. The more you practice, the more familiar you will be with your content, which will reduce the need for text- and bullet point-heavy presentations. Practicing moves you away from the natural inclination to include lots of text on your slides.

Practicing is not sitting at your desk and silently thinking about what you plan to say for each slide. Practicing—or perhaps, better put, rehearsing—involves standing up, holding your presentation clicker, and speaking aloud. Close your office door, silence your phone, and disengage from email and social media. Treat the first couple of times through as an opportunity to jot down notes and thoughts. Thereafter resist the urge to pause—treat your practice sessions as a dress rehearsal for your actual presentation.

As you practice, you will find the places where the presentation doesn't hold together and the concepts don't flow. This is your chance to go back to your slides and make adjustments. Maybe change the way you're talking through your equations, explaining your data, or relaying other concepts. Remember, you're not necessarily becoming more familiar with the content at this stage—you're becoming more familiar with how to *present* your content to an audience. Content familiarity and presentation familiarity are two very different concepts because, to return to our mantra, presentations are a different form of communication than written reports.

Practicing will also allow you to figure out how long it will take you to get through your content. How often have you seen a presenter on slide 14 of 52 with 5 minutes left in his hour-long talk? It's usually because the presenter hasn't practiced and is unable to anticipate how long it will take him to get through the content. We've all endured the boring, uninspiring presentation—which is already 5 minutes over the allotted time—waiting for it to end. This typically isn't because the questions were too hard or the technology didn't work. It is likely due to the speaker trying to present all the details from the research, and not having practiced to see how long it would take to go through all the material. Not every single detail from your paper needs to go in your presentation. When you're familiar enough with your content, you can even compensate for delays or other unexpected changes, because you'll know where you can speed up or slow down. Everyone in the room will be your friend if you end 10 minutes early—everyone in the room will be grumbling if you end 10 minutes late. The last thing you want is a roomful of people grumbling about the time instead of discussing your ideas.

As you prepare, instead of targeting your presentation for 100 percent of your time, aim for something short of that. If you aim for 40 or 50 minutes instead of 60, you will have more time for questions and you will be able to circle back if your audience looks confused about something you've said. It will also give you some leeway if the previous speaker on your panel goes long. While you may think this means you should always request to go first or second when you present in a conference session, I prefer to go last. Even though there is a risk I'll have less time than other participants, my final slide—which, you may remember from the previous chapter does not say "Thank You!" or "Questions?"—will remain on the screen during the 15 or 30 minutes of questions and discussion.

Practice can also help you detect any distracting patterns in your speech (most commonly, words such as *um*, *uh*, *so*, or *like*). These "filler" words—words we all use to bridge from one thought to another—can be grating on your audience and might suggest you are less knowledgeable or not confident in your material. Be aware of the volume of your voice as well; if you're not using a microphone, you will have to speak loudly enough to be heard over the air conditioning system or opening and closing doors. Project to the person in the back of the room.

The best way to catch and correct these habits is by recording yourself practicing. A video recording is probably best, and most smart phones now allow you to record videos fairly easily. However, I find that a simple audio recording (I use the VoiceNotes app on my iPhone) also works well. Admittedly, it can be embarrassing listening to yourself speak, but within a few minutes you'll get used to it and will start to notice things you can improve. The first time I listened to a recording of myself, I immediately heard my constant use of the filler word "um." I was then prepared to consciously eliminate it as I practiced further.

Recording yourself can also help you identify other verbal tics or filler phrases. For instance, if you're using "strong" to describe every statistic you present, or saying "the thing is" to preface every point. It is a good way to check that your word and language usage is appropriate for your audience (question #2 of the presentation worksheet). Talking in jargon and technical language may be perfectly fine in your department seminar or division meeting, but it can be less effective when speaking before a group of practitioners or testifying before Congress. As with everything else related to presentation design, make your audience your first priority and remember that they may not be as familiar with the topic as you.

Another advantage of recording yourself is to test how fast you're speaking. This is one of the most common mistakes presenters make, either because we're nervous (more on that below) or because we want to get through as much content as possible. Studies by cognitive psychologist Michael Gordon and others have found that adults have more difficulty recalling information when it is presented too quickly (age and background noise are also significant factors in reception). Slowing your rate of speech makes it easier for your audience to listen to you, which means they have more energy to put into thinking about your content. A slower speech rate—achieved by breathing more, adding pauses, and improving your diction—will also reduce your reliance on filler words because you won't find yourself fumbling for that next word or phase. You can also use the tempo of your speech for effect and to improve comprehension—for instance, speeding up (and increasing volume) when you are driving home a point and slowing down when you are walking through a complicated concept or equation.

Also, don't be afraid to pause. Pauses are natural parts of our everyday speech and give your audience a moment to absorb what you've said. The silence can be powerful, building tension and anticipation as your audience waits for you to make a point or reach a conclusion. I sometimes start a presentation by standing silently for a few seconds. I usually end up with everyone's attention because those who weren't initially watching are now wondering what's gone wrong.

Finally, as you practice, rehearse, and prepare, consider how you can use stories to cement your points and reinforce your take-home message. I once attended a colleague's practice seminar where she was presenting her research about low-income families' experience with government programs. She followed the standard academic-style presentation, winding her way through the data collection efforts, the calculations, and the results. After the seminar, we provided feedback on the presentation. She and members of her team told stories from some of the families they had interviewed: the challenges of taking multiple city buses to the government office, moving from shelter to shelter, and struggling to get their kids to school. Each story was gripping, interesting, and emotional. It was clear how they could improve their presentation: "Why don't you start with those stories?" The stories brought home the importance and value of their work in ways a table or a graph or bullet points simply did not.

While politicians, for example, know it's critical to make personal connections with their audience, those of us presenting in academic fields often forget the importance of doing so. Stories can help you connect with your audience on an emotional level, and will stay with them long after you're done speaking. Stories about how and why you became interested in your research topic, or some data or survey challenges you faced, can help motivate your presentation and engage your audience emotionally.

Your stories should fit the context of your presentation. Don't force stories that have no purpose or relationship to your content. Keep your stories short. Use them to clarify or support a point, and then move on. Don't be constrained by only the things that have happened in your professional life. Experiences with your family or friends, things you have read or watched, or the work of your colleagues can all be used in your presentation.

To recap, practice, practice, practice your presentation. Your presentation will only improve as you practice. Prepare to speak for 70–80 percent of your allotted time, so you can take questions and adapt if things are running late. Make an audio or video recording of your presentation—check for filler words and phrases, ensure your word choice is right for your audience, and make sure you're not speaking too quickly. Work stories into your presentation so you can connect your work to why people should care.

DELIVERING YOUR PRESENTATION

Practicing your presentation over and over is a good way to calm your nerves, but it probably can't eliminate your anxiety altogether. Being nervous when you give a presentation is completely normal, and even good because it suggests you actually care about whether you do a good job. While being nervous isn't a bad thing, being too nervous can make you sound shaky and unsure of your content.

That nervous feeling is your body's "fight or flight" response, dictated by the surge of adrenaline in your body, which is controlled by the hypothalamus in your brain. Your breathing gets faster, your pupils dilate, and your muscles contract, causing you to compromise your posture and slump. Because it's part of your body's natural chemistry, you can't simply "control" nervousness, but there are strategies to help calm yourself:

▸ Back to our familiar friend: Practice. Focus on what you can control before your presentation. Become as familiar as possible with your material so that you will worry less about making a mistake.
▸ Stretch your arms up and breathe deeply. This will trigger a relaxation response in your hypothalamus. With her colleagues, Amy Cuddy, a social psychologist at the Harvard Business School, has shown that this and other "power poses"—raising your arms above your head or crossing your arms across your chest—can change your chemical physiology and make you more calm and confident.
▸ Arrive early. If you show up early to your talk, you can address any technical or logistical challenges that might give you anxiety (more on this in the next chapter). There's nothing worse than rushing to set up and finding out that you don't have the right adapter to connect the projector to your computer.
▸ Exercise. Go for a walk, for a run, or to the gym. Try doing some stretching, yoga, or meditation. These activities can also help change your body chemistry and reduce your anxiety.

▶ Visualize your presentation from start to end. Psychologist James Driskell and his colleagues reviewed thirty-five studies with more than 3,200 participants to show that sitting quietly without moving and picturing yourself performing a task successfully significantly improves performance.

Nerves can also lead us to apologize, unnecessarily, for a malfunctioning projector, a cold room, or a session running late. I find that apologies—especially for things not under your control (such as the host's or audience's expectations)—set a tone of doubt or hesitation. These are the exact things you don't want your audience to feel as you launch into your content. Be confident in your material and your approach. There are sure to be times when your presentation falls flat, your slides fail to effectively capture your message, or your audience doesn't buy into your ideas. Anything can happen, but don't start your presentation by setting yourself up for failure. Be confident in your ideas and content, and your audience is more likely to follow you.

Another possible strategy you can use if you're really nervous is to talk to some of the people in the audience before your presentation begins. Introduce yourself to some of the audience members and ask about their research interests. One-on-one conversations can calm your nerves because they are easier than presenting to an entire room. Forming personal connections before your presentation can also give you people to make eye contact with periodically as you deliver your presentation. As the presenter, your goal is to connect with your audience, and by chatting with people before your talk starts, you can better foster these connections.

EMOTIONS MATTER

Your audience *will* pick up on your emotions. If you are self-assured, they will have confidence in you and your content; if you are nervous or unsure, they may be unconvinced; and if you are bored of giving the same talk for the hundredth time, they will likely be bored as well. Many in your audience will be hearing your presentation for the first time, so deliver your message with as much enthusiasm and confidence as you can muster. Remember, regardless of where you are or how you feel, your presentation is not about you—it is about your audience.

Aside from your slides, the main focus will be on you. Since your slides are now simple, clear, and fully unified with the content you're presenting, the audience should be able to spend much more time looking at and listening to you, rather than reading and staring at your slides. So you'll want to put some thought into how you position and present yourself throughout your presentation.

Just as most of us go with the default color palette or slide design in PowerPoint, we also tend to stick with the default presentation setup—standing behind a podium, which in most cases sits off to one side while the slides take center stage. In this default scenario the podium creates a physical barrier between you and your audience, especially if you place your computer on top of it. Instead, I recommend trying to make yourself—not your slides—the physical center of attention. This generally means trying to stay in the center of the room, or just off to the side of the screen. If you arrive early, you can work with your host to move the podium, and replace it with a small table or chair for your computer. Another option is to simply stand to the side of the podium rather than behind it, with your computer angled toward you if needed (so you can see the slides or your notes). When positioning your computer, be aware of where your cords and notes sit. You don't want to trip over a power cable that stretches across the floor, or knock your notes to the floor. Remember, this is *your* presentation and you've spent a considerable amount of time getting ready, so be as comfortable as you can with the room arrangement when it's time to actually present.

As you're giving your presentation, be mindful of how you're holding yourself and how you're engaging with the audience. Specifically:

▶ Maintain good posture. Keep your back straight and your chest and arms open. Based on research by Cuddy and other researchers in a variety of fields, you may feel more confident when you stand like this, and your audience will perceive you as being more self-assured (Cuddy discusses many of these studies in her book *Presence*). But don't overthink this: don't worry too much about exactly where you're standing or where your arms are or how long you've looked at one side of the room. Just use your best judgment and be comfortable—this will make you will feel better, which in turn will make your audience feel better.

▶ Find a good place for the microphone. This is especially important if you're using a lavalier microphone (sometimes called a lapel microphone) where the microphone clips to your shirt or jacket and the transmitter (usually about the size of a deck of cards) goes in your pocket or clips to your belt. Work with the audio technician and find a comfortable set up. If you're using a handheld microphone, figure out which hand you will use to hold the microphone and which one will hold the slide clicker.

▸ Smile, and look like you're enjoying yourself (and hopefully you are!). Studies have found that smiling can help reduce stress, and lower your heart rate and blood pressure. People are also inclined to imitate facial expressions, so if you're smiling, it's likely your audience will smile back. Let your personality shine through—your presentation is a means of communication and your personality can help drive your audience's engagement, and adoption, of your content.

▸ Use small, natural gestures. Walk if there is space, but make it purposeful—you don't want this to look like pacing, so just a few steps will do. Don't be afraid to walk over to the screen and point to a section of your slide. I usually add an arrow or circle or boldface to my slides to help highlight a specific point of focus, but sometimes you just need to physically walk to the screen and point to an important number or object.

▸ Dress well. We live in a casual age and it can be difficult to gauge when to dress formally and when to dress more casually. Try to be aware of the basic dress code of the organization or conference where you are speaking, and try to match it. When in doubt, opt for more formal dress over more casual. Your audience won't look askance if you're dressed more formally than they are, but they might if you're less so. Take your bulky set of keys and your phone out of your pocket and put them somewhere safe, especially if you're giving a formal presentation. If you do keep your phone with you, be sure to turn off the sound.

▸ Maintain eye contact. Try to connect with each person in the room (especially if it's a small room) so that they feel like you are talking just to them. You will come across as conversational, which will automatically engage your audience.

▸ Finally, consider how you can make your audience feel as if they are part of the presentation and embrace the subject. Good posture and eye contact encourages this kind of engagement, but there may also be times—especially in longer presentations—when having your audience *do* something can aid you in delivering your message. You might simply ask your audience to raise their hands or call out answers in response to a question. You can also suggest that your audience use an online social media platform such as Twitter to ask questions, respond to a poll, or share their thoughts (this can be especially effective if your presentation is being streamed live or otherwise shared beyond those physically in the room). Be sure to provide your audience with a hashtag or some other identifier so that they can find the discussion thread.

▶ ▶ ▶ ▶ ▶

Your presentation is about you, not about your slides. While much of this book is dedicated to helping you create better slides with less text and more images, your presentation is ultimately about you and your research. Be sure to practice your presentation—knowing the results of your regressions is not the same as knowing how to verbally communicate these findings to an audience. Practicing will also help eliminate your use of filler words and the need for slides where you've listed all of the points you want to make and numbers you want to share. You will be prepared to deliver an effective presentation that will engage your audience with your work.

THREE THINGS TO REMEMBER ABOUT PRESENTING

1. **Visualize.** See yourself delivering a successful presentation. Incorporate other relaxation strategies to help you calm your nerves.
2. **Unify.** Pull your content, your appearance and posture, and any stories you might tell together into a consistent theme.
3. **Focus.** Practice, practice, practice. Dedicate some focused time on preparing to actually give your presentation.

THE TECHNICAL NITTY-GRITTY

E ven a decade ago, most presentations required only a speaker, a lectern, and an audience— the addition of a blackboard or transparency projector was about as complicated as it might get. But today, even simple presentations require an array of technologies—a computer, a projector, various cords and wires, a clicker, and more. Being aware of what you need and common issues that could arise are your best defense against dreaded "technical difficulties."

Preparing in advance for the technical ins and outs of your presentation will ensure everything looks the way you expect and that things run as smoothly as possible. From preparing your own speaker notes to deciding whether to provide your audience with a handout, to knowing what cables and cords you might need to hook up your computer, this chapter covers the final details you need to make your presentation flow seamlessly.

USING NOTES

If you're used to relying on the bullet points on your slide as prompts, you may worry that you might forget an important point if you use slides containing less text and more images than usual. You can alleviate these concerns by using the *Notes* feature of your presentation software or by using a hard copy of your notes on paper or index cards; some presenters put their notes on a tablet or phone. Some presentation authors discourage using visible notes, arguing your audience shouldn't know you're relying on these cues. Personally, I would rather use notes and be confident that I won't omit important content than look casual and off-the-cuff—and forget to mention a key point.

I prefer using digital notes, which are usually available in the *Notes* feature of my slide software (both PowerPoint and Keynote have a window for notes located directly below the slide). Your audience can't see that you're referring to your notes, and you can usually fit more in the *Notes* pane on the computer than you can on an index card.

In PowerPoint, as with most presentation software tools, the *Presenter View* (accessible under the *View* menu) shows you the current slide, the next slide, and space at the bottom for your notes. Your audience will only see the current slide. You may also see a timer on the screen that can help you track your presentation. For example, if you've practiced, you will know that you should be in the "Challenges for Girls' Education in Developing Countries" section 20 minutes into your presentation. If you've missed that mark, you can speed up or slow down. You may need to modify the settings of your operating system or slide software to use the presenter view on your computer without connecting to a projector.

Unfortunately, using the *Notes* feature also forces you to rely on your computer. In some cases, the computer may be located far from where you are actually standing to present. Another potential obstacle is the conference organizer or the chair of the conference panel may want to load all the presentations onto a single computer and mandate the use of a preset display. This can be a problem if the preset display is not compatible with your *Notes* feature. As a failsafe in case one (or more) of these issues occurs, it's a good idea to have your slide notes available in a different form, possibly printed or written out or even on your phone. Remember the more you practice the less you will need to rely on your notes.

Whether you go analog or digital, keep your notes short and concise. Use them to direct your thoughts and remind you of the major points. Also, this is where bullet points are okay! You want to be able to glance at your computer screen or the cards in your hand and be reminded of each point, but you don't want to depend on them so heavily that you're reading the text word-for-word. Reciting a prepared presentation can result in your speech sounding stilted and robotic, and it can also make you sound less confident in your material. It also means you will be looking down while you speak instead of facing your audience and engaging with them directly. This is especially true in small rooms, conferences, and less formal atmospheres, where the natural interaction between you and the audience is disrupted when you read your remarks word-for-word. Reading a presentation can occasionally work—consider the State of the Union address, for example—but for many presenters, this approach is too formal and less personable.

ASPECT RATIOS

The dimensions of your slides can have important consequences influencing how they appear when projected. The aspect ratio (the ratio of a slide's width to its height) of slides in most presentation software programs has typically been "4:3" (the slide is 33 percent wider than it is tall). This measurement stems from the standard size of an analog TV screen. A traditional projector—the projector that sits on the table in the seminar room or is mounted to the ceiling in the classroom—will usually use a 4:3 ratio. However, newer projectors, widescreen TVs, and large computer monitors are more likely to have a "16:9" aspect ratio (the screen is 78 percent wider than it is tall). In response, newer presentation programs offer the widescreen format as the default; in PowerPoint 2013 and 2016, for example, the default slide format is 16:9, and Keynote allows the user to choose either a Standard or Wide format upon opening a new presentation.

The aspect ratio of your slides, and the projector you use, will determine the overall appearance of your slides on the screen. Because of this shift toward widescreen projectors and screens, it's probably a good idea to create your slides in a 16:9 layout. Ideally, your host or conference organizer will be able to tell you what kind of projector they use, but alas, this is not always the case. Showing a 4:3 slide on a 16:9 screen is not the end of the world—you will usually see two black columns on either side of the image (known as "pillarboxing"). If you show a 16:9 slide on a 4:3 screen, you will likely see two black rows above and below

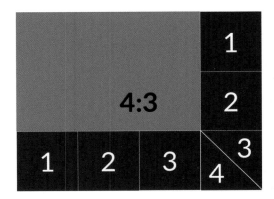
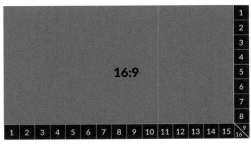

Typical slide dimensions, 4×3 and 16×9 (after Presentitude, 2014)

the image (known as "letterboxing"). If you find yourself in either predicament, just accept it and move on. Do not try to edit your slides right before you start speaking. You'll find most people won't mind, especially if your slides are already captivating and visual.

If you do have time to convert a presentation from a 4:3 aspect ratio to a 16:9 aspect ratio, or vice versa, you may find that simply changing the slide dimensions will stretch your images and distort your slide layouts. Newer versions of PowerPoint have gotten much better at not stretching the images as much (though they still stretch background images from the Master slide), but instead add space to the left and right edge of the slide, so some slight adjustments may be necessary. In some tools (and certainly in older versions of PowerPoint), your images may stretch when you convert from one slide dimension to another. I've added the white circle in the image below to demonstrate how simply changing the aspect ratio of the slide can stretch an image. To adjust the distorted images in the new layout, you can create a new presentation file and copy-and-paste each image from the old file to the new. Alternatively, you can adjust the size of your now-distorted images by reverting the aspect ratio of each image back to their original dimensions. (In PowerPoint, you can quickly resize an image by right-clicking on it and selecting the *Size and Position* menu. Then click the *Height* box and click up once and down once. As long as the *Lock Aspect Ratio* checkbox is checked, changing the scale by one step up and then back will fix the image. On computers running the Windows operating system, the dialog menu will not close once you're done editing the image, so you can leave it open and go from one image to the next quickly and easily.)

Converting an image from 4x3 to 16x9 can stretch or distort the image.
(Photo by Padurariu Alexandru, Unsplash.com)

There are also programs such as Resize (*http://pptools.com/resize/index.html*), Photoshop, and iResizer that you can use to convert the aspect ratio of your images.

TECHNICAL SET-UP AND TOOLS

There will certainly be occasions when you will not be able to use your own computer to show your slides and in those cases, your host or conference organizer is going to want your slides to be put on a central computer. Depending on the size of the file—especially if you're including images and videos—you may have difficulty transferring it to the organizer. Cloud-based storage services like Box, Dropbox, Google Drive, and OneDrive are making it easier to share large files. If you have time prior to speaking, you can also use an external hard drive or USB key to transfer your files. Irrespective of the technology you choose to share your files, ask the host to run a quick test with your slides to make sure things look correct.

A primary advantage of arriving early for your presentation is that you have plenty of time to confirm the slides project the way you like, to ensure the resolution looks good, and to arrange yourself and your technology. You'll be able to decide where you want to stand and where your computer will go, and have the chance to assess and prepare whatever else you may need. If you want to be as prepared as possible for the various venues and locations you may encounter, then there are a number of tools you may want to have on hand:

1. **Projector adapters.** In the past, most computers hooked up to projectors through the Video Graphics Array (VGA) input, a port that sort of looks like a parallelogram with about 15 different holes. However, newer computers use all sorts of high-definition input options, including Digital Visual Input (DVI), High-Definition Multimedia Interface (HDMI), Digital Visual Interface (DVI), Universal Serial Bus (USB), and USB-C ports that connect to different kinds of projectors and televisions. These high-definition inputs are quickly becoming the norm as they match the new high-definition screens and projectors (Apple computers and newer PCs do not have VGA ports anymore). There should already be a cord from the projector (many modern projectors will have both VGA and HDMI outputs) or television to connect to your computer (you probably just have to trust that your host has a projector and cable from the projector). (Some professional speakers will bring their own projector with them to avoid inadequacies.) Connecting the projector to your computer will also depend on the ports

available on your computer, so understand what your computer allows. For example, if you only have an HDMI port, you may want to purchase a VGA-to-HDMI adapter just to be safe. Adapters come in all shapes and sizes, and some will have multiple options bundled into a single adapter. In general, adapters run from about $5 to $50.

2. **Adapter extension cord.** Sometimes you will want to move your computer farther than the reach of the existing projector cables. In these cases, it is helpful to have an extension cord that will give you the freedom to place your computer wherever you are most comfortable. These extension cords run about $10, but may be pricier depending on the input needs for your specific computer. Also remember, when traveling overseas, you may need a separate power adapter.

3. **Clicker.** These handheld devices move your slides forward or backward. Some offer a "blank screen" or "breaker" button that will show a completely black or white screen. Most also have a laser pointer, though if you've embraced the overall message of this book of simplifying and decluttering your slides—and using highlighting elements such as colors, circles, or arrows—you shouldn't need it. Really good clickers start at about $40. These clickers usually communicate with the computer via USB, so if you are not using your own computer, be sure to check that the computer you are using allows you to connect a USB device.

4. **Batteries.** Always keep some backups! Expect your clicker to die at just the wrong moment. I had this happen once during a presentation. I made some wisecrack about always being prepared, broke out a new pair of double-As and kept right on going.

5. **Power extension cord.** I usually try to charge my laptop battery the night before a presentation, but if I'm giving a full-day workshop or if I can't charge the battery before my presentation, I'll bring an extension cord with me. This is especially important if you are using an older computer where the battery may run out more quickly.

6. **Sound extension cord.** If you plan on using sound or video with sound in your presentation, you may want to include a sound extension cord, just in case the projector doesn't have one or there is a separate sound system in the room. All you need is an extension cord with a female connector (to connect to the original cord) and a male connector (to connect to your computer). These are relatively inexpensive, usually less than $10.

7. **Portable speaker.** If you're using sound in your presentation and the room is small enough, you may also want to carry a small speaker. Mobile speakers are fairly affordable, small, and can project sound extremely well.

8. **Surge protector.** If you're worried about power surges, get yourself a decent surge protector. They are not that costly and if you have one with multiple ports, and are sitting at a common area at your conference, you'll be a hero.

9. **USB drive.** Backup your presentation on a USB drive, just in case. I save my files in both PowerPoint and PDF format, so that I can run them without difficulty on another computer. Remember, if you're using non-standard fonts and haven't embedded them in your PowerPoint file, a PDF file is the best way to ensure they look right on another system. You can also backup your files using a cloud storage service.

10. **Tape.** In some venues, the microphone, power, VGA, HDMI, or sound cords, may dangle off the edge of the table or podium and become dislodged from your computer. There may also be cords crossing the floor where you plan to speak, creating a dangerous (or potentially comical) situation. Pack a roll of masking tape so you can secure these occupational hazards.

11. **Dry erase markers or chalk.** Depending on where you speak, you may have access to a whiteboard or chalkboard. If you are a teacher, writing on a board may come naturally to you, so don't be afraid to use it, especially if it can be used to help answer questions. It's incredibly frustrating when you pick up a dry erase marker that doesn't work, or walk up to the chalkboard to find no chalk. So if you plan to write on a board, or plan on seizing the opportunity should it present itself, pack some markers and a piece of chalk in your bag.

Altogether, you can pack a bag of presentation tools for around $100. Most presenters won't need things like portable speakers, surge protectors, or extension cords, so the outlay could be considerably less.

Once you're all set up, take a minute to make the computer you're using "presentation ready." When your computer is connected to the Internet, you may end up with all kinds of distractions popping up from email arriving in your inbox and message alerts from Twitter or Facebook, to software update notifications and other random items. The simple solution is to turn off your Internet connection until the presentation is over. However, you may need the connection for your presentation—for example, if you're giving a demonstration or streaming a video (one reason I prefer to download videos to my computer is to avoid this reliance on the Internet; recall chapter 8). Quit—really quit, don't just minimize—any programs you don't absolutely need. Also, depending on your computer, you may need to adjust your power settings to ensure your computer does not shut off or go to sleep during a period of inactivity (for example, during the question and answer period). I also recommend boot-ing up your computer well before your presentation—even hours before. There are times when your computer will automatically start installing updates that can take a really long time to process. You don't want to have to sit there and wait anxiously for your computer to finish installing and restarting as people are filing into the room. I will also quickly click through my entire presentation before I give it, just to be sure everything looks as planned, and animations and videos operate as expected.

Try to become knowledgeable about the culture of the audience to whom you'll be speak-ing. Maybe you're traveling to a country for the first time or speaking at an internal meeting in a specialized firm. What is the culture like? Will they interrupt you to ask questions? Do people tend to arrive on the later side? If a full-day conference or meeting, will there be a need for long breaks for snacks or prayers? Will there be a casual or working lunch? Hope-fully, you can have a conversation with your host to ask these sorts of questions, all with the effect of keeping your audience in mind. Again, the better prepared you are before you ar-rive, the better you will be able to anticipate any challenges and fine-tune your experience.

DELIVERING ONLINE PRESENTATIONS

Online meetings and presentations have become increasingly common. Authors Ruth Clark and Richard Mayer report that the share of all educational training delivered on the com-puter (including on CDs, Intranets, and the Internet) grew from 11 percent in 2001 to nearly 40 percent in 2010. Delivering online presentations and instruction differs from speaking in person because you may not be able to interact with your audience in the same way—you can't read their reactions, quickly answer questions, or hear the laughter from your jokes. While your audience may feel uncomfortable nodding off or looking at their phones during your lunchtime seminar, there's little shame in checking email or browsing the Internet dur-ing a webinar when they are sitting alone in their office.

Due to these potential interaction and attention challenges, you might consider adjusting your slides for the webinar environment. You may *want* to include some text on your slides be-cause it will force your audience to read the slide and pay attention to your content. However, the same rules pertaining to distractions apply, so continue to focus your audience's attention. Let them know when you are going to be quiet for a moment to allow them time to read the slide or do an exercise. I find taking breaks for exercises or asking questions (and having the audience speak up or use a chat box) during a webinar is a great engagement strategy.

I strongly recommend you test your slides in the webinar platform prior to delivering your presentation. Some webinar tools will not render unique fonts or high-resolution images very well. If you plan on giving numerous webinars, I also recommend getting yourself a pair of quality headphones and a good microphone; I like Blue microphones, but there are many other good ones available on the market.

There are lots of online delivery platforms including Adobe Connect, Google Hangouts, Goto Webinar, Skype, WebEx, and Zeetings. Your choice will depend on a variety of factors including the layout of the interface and how many people you expect to attend.

HANDOUTS AND SHARING SLIDES

As you move the detailed numbers, estimates, and long passages of text off your slide, you may still find you have specific details excluded from your slide that you want to share with your audience. If so, think carefully about when and how you make these available. I often see presenters provide printed copies of their entire presentation for the audience. It usually doesn't take long for the audience to start glancing through the print outs and stop paying attention to the speaker.

Depending on the audience size and the layout of the room, you can delay distributing the handout until it needs to be referenced. If the document is going to be used throughout the presentation or it's just easier to pass it around at the beginning, tell your audience when you are going to refer to it and why they'll need it. Hopefully, this will discourage them from looking at the handout until you're ready to go through it with them.

In this context, handouts are distinct from the entire written report; only include a detailed table or two, or a page of equations. If a larger packet of information is required, the use of page numbers can be helpful because you can help navigate the audience through the pages of the handout. Only include as much detail as you think the audience needs. This minimizes the risk they will stop listening to you and instead read the document. Handouts can be useful, but continue to implement the principles described earlier: Focus your audience's attention on important details, and don't just dump documents on their laps because you can. Integrate what you are going to say and show on the screen with the information specified in the handouts, and keep a unified aesthetic between them.

Another alternative is to add the more complex, detailed slides after your final slide. These "appendix" slides can be especially useful if you've anticipated questions (recall question 10 from the worksheet in chapter 1) that will need supplementary explanations or more detailed information. If you need to use this additional material during your presentation, you can always stop projecting your slides for a moment and advance to these appendix slides. In many presentation tools, you can insert links into your presentation that when clicked will bring you directly to the appropriate slide. The LaTeX-based Beamer tool makes this especially easy, but you can also do this in PowerPoint by using the *Place in this Document* option in the hyperlink menu.

Many of us like to make our slides available after our presentations, for audience members to recall what they heard and so those who weren't there can review. I am aware that if you adopt the suggestions in this book—less text, more images—people who do not attend your presentation are going to have a hard time understanding what transpired by looking at your slides alone. A friend of mine once asked a presenter to send him slides for a presentation he was unable to attend. The presenter happily sent him the slides, which turned out to be a series of pictures of mountains and dogs with minimal text. "These slides aren't that helpful," my friend emailed the presenter, to which she responded, partly tongue-in-cheek, "Well, next time, you should attend the talk."

There is no magic solution for creating a presentation intended to serve two naturally incompatible purposes—it can't be done well. The most time-consuming way to address this incompatibility is to create two different slide decks: One that you use when you present to your audience and another document for sharing. A slightly easier approach is to create a companion document that you share along with the slides, which includes information presented in your talk.

If you wish to integrate the two forms together, you can use the *Notes* feature of your slide software. In this approach, you may want to replace the notes used to prompt your presentation with added text and details to create more of a narrative for your reader. If you plan to share the actual presentation file, you can also place text boxes off to the side of the actual slide. They won't appear on the screen when you present, but the reader will see them when they open the file on their computer.

Instead of sharing the actual slides, you can also create a separate document for your reader. You can easily create this in a word processing tool by pasting your slides into the document and adding text around them. In PowerPoint, you can use the *Notes* option in the *Print* menu. The output will create a document with an image of your slide at the top of the page and your notes just below. In addition, you can style the notes as you would in a word processing program. Saving ("printing") the file as a PDF will allow you to share it with your readers as a more unified document.

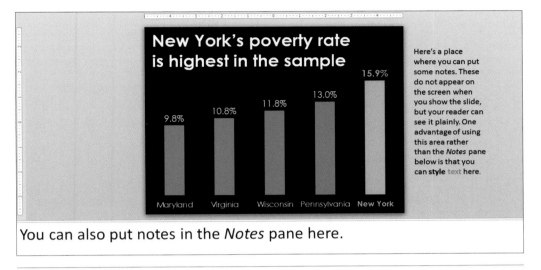

Add notes or explanatory text in the Notes pane or off to the side of the slide.

Finally, instead of doing any additional typing or redesigning, you can make an audio or video recording of your actual presentation, and share or post the pair together (you may wish to inform your audience that you are doing so). Just remember that once you share or post your presentation, it can be widely distributed without your control. If you use this strategy, you may want to have a recording tool that produces a high-quality audio file. Personally, I have found that my computer or phone will capture audio and video recordings with sufficient quality for this purpose.

▸ ▸ ▸ ▸ ▸

Don't let the hard work of preparing your content and slides go to waste by not preparing for the actual job of presenting your material. Prepare yourself and your computer by turning off unnecessary computer programs and alerts, and by knowing which cords and adapters you need. Remember, it is important to arrive early. Arriving early allows you to set up your hardware and become familiar with the room. You might still be nervous, but if you arrive early, you can at least be confident your technology will work (well, at least to the best of your abilities—there is always the unknown malfunction) and you can focus on effectively delivering your presentation.

THREE THINGS TO REMEMBER ABOUT THE NITTY-GRITTY

1. **Visualize.** Try to know what kind of screen or projector you will be using. It's not the end of the world to project 4:3 slides on a widescreen projector, but if you know you'll be using a widescreen projector beforehand, you can design your slides accordingly.
2. **Unify.** If you need to use handouts, make sure their appearance (and content!) are consistent with your slides and what you plan to say.
3. **Focus.** Prepare for your technological needs. Know what adapters or inputs your computer might require and try to find out what is necessary for the room you are presenting in.

CONCLUSIONS

I hope you are convinced that creating more visual slides—with less text, bullets, and dense graphs and tables—is a better and more efficient way to communicate with your audience. Filling slides with sentence after sentence, number after number, and line after line forces your audience to work too hard while you are speaking. They will pay more attention to all those little details and less attention to you. These specifics are better suited for your written report.

As you prepare for your next presentation, don't hurry to your computer, boot up your presentation software, and start typing. Think carefully about your message and how you want to share this information with your audience. Know precisely what you would like your audience to do with your content, and use your presentation as a means to go beyond what they will get from your written report. Your presentation is your opportunity to give your audience something that they can't necessarily get from the written word: You.

So remember:

Visualize your content, from the dense table of statistics to the header slides that help you transition from one section to another. Your audience is much more likely to recognize and remember your content if you present it visually.

Unify what you say with what you show. Be consistent across your slide design and your presentation style. Doing so will reduce the amount of mental energy your audience will spend as you move from one slide or section to the next. The result will be an audience that spends more time engaging with you, your content, and your message.

Focus your audience's attention on each point, each number, and each fact you want them to take away. You don't need to present them with everything at once. Control what they see and when they see it by focusing their attention where you want it.

A presentation is a fundamentally different form of communication than what you write down and publish in a journal, report, or blog post. Bring your audience along with you on the journey of your presentation, so that they will remember you and your presentation, and act on the content you deliver.

FURTHER READINGS

I f you want to further enhance your presentation design and delivery skills, there are a number of great books, blogs, and tools available. I've already highlighted some of the better color, font, and data visualization tools earlier in the book, and I maintain a current list on the book's website (*www.policyviz.com/better-presentations*). Here, I list some of my favorite books on presentation skills and design, with additional presentation design resources included on the book's website.

MICHAEL ALLEY. In *The Craft of Scientific Presentations,* Alley lays out a particular approach to scientific presentation delivery, and includes a long list of scientific evidence for his approach from the psychology, neuroscience, and education fields.

RICK ALTMAN. More PowerPoint specific than other books on the market, Altman's *Why Most PowerPoint Presentations Suck and How You Can Make Them Better* shows detailed steps and approaches in PowerPoint for creating better presentations. He also includes a number of before-and-after remakes.Scott Berkun. Author of a number of books on innovation and creativity, his *Confessions of a Public Speaker* focuses on his practical presentation delivery techniques. This is not a book on slide design but instead focuses on presentation delivery. It covers how to deal with nerves, how to manage a tough room, and what to do when things go wrong.

MATT CARTER. One of the few books on presentations for the sciences, Carter's book, *Designing Science Presentations: A Visual Guide to Figures, Papers, Slides, Posters, and More* provides good insight on how to present scientific information in a variety of formats.

NANCY DUARTE. Author of several books on presentation skills and design including *Slide:ology* and *Resonate* (as well as her perhaps less-known *Harvard Business Review Guide to Persuasive Presentations*). Duarte's books are modern classics in the presentation field. Her books primarily focus on how to create better slides and give better presentations.

CARMINE GALLO. Gallo's book, *The Secrets of Steve Jobs* dissects the Apple co-founder's presentations. He shows how Jobs' approach and design are effective ways to present information and describes how they can be successfully applied to improve your work. In *Talk Like TED: The 9 Public-Speaking Secrets of the World's Top Minds,* Gallo breaks down the strategy involved for hundreds of successful TED talks. His latest book, *The Storyteller's Secret: From TED Speakers to Business Legends, Why Some Ideas Catch On and Other Don't,* covers the storytelling strategies of business leaders and speakers.

STEVEN KOSSLYN. A cognitive neuroscientist and author of several books on psychology and communication, Kosslyn's *Better PowerPoint* focuses on quick steps to improve presentations you already have, and ways to improve new presentations.

GARR REYNOLDS. Author of modern classics, *Presentation Zen, Presentation Zen: Design*, and *The Naked Presenter*, Reynolds's books focus on basic presentation skills and design. He is a proponent of simple, clean slides that more effectively present information with before and after examples.

ECHO SWINFORD and JULIE TERBERG. Their *Building PowerPoint Templates* is probably the best book on creating themes and templates in PowerPoint. It teaches you to build PowerPoint presentations with consistent branding and design, which can be shared between collaborators or across an organization.

ROBIN WILLIAMS. Author of *The Non-Designer's Design Book*, a primer on design. It is perfect for those needing an introduction to color, font, layout, and other aspects of design.

REFERENCES

Supplementary references are available on the book's website at *www.policyviz.com/better-presentations*.

Alley, Michael. 2013. *The Craft of Scientific Presentations: Critical Steps to Succeed and Critical Errors to Avoid.* New York: Springer.

Altman, Rick. 2012. *Why Most PowerPoint Presentations Suck and How You Can Make Them Better.* Pleasanton, CA: Harvest.

Aron, Laudan Y., Lisa Dubay, Elaine Waxman, and Steven Martin. 2015. *To Understand Climbing Death Rates Among White Americans, Look to Women* (blog). *The Urban Institute.* November 10, 2015. http://www.urban.org/urban-wire/understand-climbing-death-rates-among-white-americans-look-women.

Berkun, Scott. 2011. *Confessions of a Public Speaker.* Sebastopol, CA: O'Reilly Media.

Bernstein, Lenny and Joel Achenbach. "A Group of Middle-Aged Whites in the U.S. Is Dying at a Startling Rate." *Washington Post*, November 2, 2015.

Borkin, Michelle, Krzysztof Z. Gajos, Amanda Peters, Dimitrios Mitsouras, Simone Melchionna, Frank J. Rybicki, Charles L. Feldman, and Hanspeter Pfister. 2011. "Evaluation of artery visualizations for heart disease diagnosis." *Visualization and Computer Graphics, IEEE Transactions* 17(12): 2479–88.

Bureau of Labor Statistics. 2016a. "Labor Force Statistics from the Current Population Survey." Extracted May 2016. http://www.bls.gov/cps/.

Bureau of Labor Statistics. 2016b. "Job Openings and Labor Turnover Survey." Extracted May 2016. http://www.bls.gov/jlt/.

Cairo, Alberto. 2012. *The Functional Art: An Introduction to Information Graphics and Visualization.* Berkeley, CA: New Riders.

—— 2016. *The Truthful Art: Data, Charts, and Maps for Communication.* Berkeley, CA: New Riders.

Camões, Jorge. 2016. *Data at Work: Best practices for creating effective charts and information graphics in Microsoft Excel.* Berkeley, CA: New Riders.

Carter, Matt. 2013. *Designing Science Presentations: A Visual Guide to Figures, Papers, Slides, Posters, and More.* London: Academic Press.

Case, Anne, and Angus Deaton. 2015. "Rising morbidity and mortality in midlife among white non-Hispanic Americans in the 21st century." *Proceedings of the National Academy of Sciences of the United States of America* 112 (49): 15078–83.

Clark, Ruth C., and Richard E. Mayer. 2011. *E-Learning and the Science of Instruction: Proven Guidelines for Consumers and Designers of Multimedia Learning,* 3rd Edition. San Francisco, CA: Pfeiffer.

College Board. 2015. *Trends in College Pricing 2015.* http://trends.collegeboard.org/sites/default/files/trends-college-pricing-web-final-508-2.pdf.

Congressional Budget Office. 2014. "An Update to the Budget and Economic Outlook: 2014 to 2024." https://www.cbo.gov/publication/45653.

Cuddy, Amy J.C., Caroline A. Wilmuth, and Dana R. Carney. 2012. "The Benefit of Power Posing Before a High-Stakes Social Evaluation." *Harvard Business School Working Paper No. 13- 027.* September.

Cuddy, Amy. 2015. *Presence: Bringing your Boldest Self to your Biggest Challenges.* New York: Little, Brown.

Dehaene, Stanislas. 2009. *Reading in the Brain: The New Science of How We Read.* New York: Penguin.

Driskell, James E., Carolyn Copper, and Aidan Moran. 1994. "Does Mental Practice Enhance Performance?" *Journal of Applied Psychology* 79 (4): 481.

Duarte, Nancy. 2008. *Slide:ology: The Art and Science of Creating Great Presentations.* Sebastopol, CA: O'Reilly Media.

——. 2010. *Resonate: Present Visual Stories that Transform Audiences.* Hoboken, NJ: Wiley.

——. 2012. *HBR Guide to Persuasive Presentations (HBR Guide Series).* Boston, MA: Harvard Business Review Press.

Evergreen, Stephanie. 2016. *Effective Data Visualization: The Right Chart for the Right Data.* Thousand Oaks, CA: Sage.

Few, Stephen. 2007. "Save the Pies for Dessert." *Visual Business Intelligence Newsletter* (August). https://www.perceptualedge.com/articles/visual_business_intelligence/save_the_pies_for_dessert.pdf.

——. 2009. *Now You See It: Simple Visualization Techniques for Quantitative Analysis.* Oakland, CA: Analytics Press.

——. 2012. *Show Me the Numbers: Designing Tables and Graphs to Enlighten,* 2nd edition. Burlingame, CA: Analytics Press.

Gallo, Carmine. 2011. *The Presentation Secrets of Steve Jobs: How to Be Insanely Great in Front of Any Audience.* New York: McGraw Hill.

Gallo, Carmine. 2015. *Talk Like TED: The 9 Public-Speaking Secrets of the World's Top Minds*. New York: St. Martin's Griffin.

——. 2016. *The Storyteller's Secret: From TED Speakers to Business Legends, Why Some Ideas Catch On and Others Don't*. New York: St. Martin's.

Gapminder. 2016. "Data in a Gapminder World," http://www.gapminder.org/data/.

Garner, Joanna K., Michael Alley, Allen F. Gaudelli, and Sarah E. Zappe. 2009. "Common Use of PowerPoint versus the Assertion-Evidence Structure: A Cognitive Psychology Perspective." *Technical Communication* 56 (4): 331–45.

Gegenfurtner, Karl R., Lindsay T. Sharpe, and B.B. Boycott. 2001. *Color Vision: From Genes to Perception*. New York: Cambridge University Press.

Gordon, Michael S., Meredyth Daneman, and Bruce A. Schneider. 2009. "Comprehension of Speeded Discourse by Younger and Older Listeners." *Experimental Aging Research* 35: 277–96.

Groeger, Lena. 2016. "How Typography Can Save Your Life." *ProPublica*. May 11. https://www.propublica.org/article/how-typography-can-save-your-life.

Hartley, James and Ivor K. Davies. 1978. "Note-taking: A critical review." *Programmed Learning and Education Technology* 15(3): 207–24.

Healey, Christopher G., and James T. Enns. 2012. "Attention and Visual Memory in Visualization and Computer Graphics." *IEEE Transactions on Visualization and Computer Graphics* 18(7): 1170–88.

Heath, Chip, and Dan Heath. 2007. *Made to Stick*. New York, NY: Random House.

Hoffler, Alan. 2015. *Presentation Sin: The Practical Guide to Stop Offending (and Start Impressing) Your Audience*. MillsWyck Communications, Kindle edition.

Johnstone, A.H. and F. Percival. 1976. "Attention Breaks in Lectures." *Education in Chemistry* 13(2): 49–50.

Kahneman, Daniel. 2013. *Thinking, Fast and Slow*. New York, NY: Farrar, Straus and Giroux.

Kawasaki, Guy. 2015. "The Minimalist Guide to Pitching." LinkedIn. (July 27). https://www.linkedin.com/pulse/minimalist-guide-pitching-guy-kawasaki.

King, Elizabeth M., and Rebecca Winthrop. 2015. "Today's Challenges for Girls' Education." *Global Economy and Development Working Paper No. 90*. Global Economy and Development, The Brookings Institution.

Kirk, Andy. 2016. *Data Visualisation: A Handbook for Data Driven Design*. Thousand Oaks, CA: Sage.

Kosara, Robert, and Drew Skau. 2016. "Judgment Error in Pie Chart Variations." *Short Paper Proceedings of the Eurographics/IEEE VGTC Symposium on Visualizations* (EuroVis): 91–95.

Kosslyn, Steven. 2010. *Better PowerPoint (R): Quick Fixes Based On How Your Audience Thinks*. New York: Oxford University Press.

Mackiewicz, Jo. 2006. "Audience Perceptions of Fonts in Projected PowerPoint Text Slides." *International Professional Communication Conference*: 68–76.

Mayer, Richard. 2009. *Multimedia Learning*. New York: Cambridge University Press.

McKeachie, Wilbert J. 1999. *McKeachie's Teaching Tips: Strategies, Research, and Theory for College and University Teachers*, 10th edition. Boston, MA: Houghton Mifflin Company.

Medina, John. 2014. *Brain Rules: Twelve Principles for Surviving and Thriving at Work, Home and School,* 2nd edition. Seattle, WA: Pear Press.

Meirelles, Isabel. 2013. *Design for Information: An Introduction to the Histories, Theories, and Best Practices Behind Effective Information Visualizations.* Beverly, MA: Rockport.

Miller, George A. 1956. "The Magical Number Seven, Plus or Minus Two: Some Limits on Our Capacity for Processing Information." *Psychological Review* 63 (2): 81–97.

NASA Ames Research Center. No date. "Designing with Luminance Contrast." *Color Usage Research Lab.* http://colorusage.arc.nasa.gov/design_lum_0.php.

Noar, Adam. 2012. *Slides Made Simple,* 2nd edition. E-book. http://presentationpanda.com/book/.

Nussbaumer Knaflic, Cole. 2015. *Storytelling with Data: A Data Visualization Guide for Business Professionals.* Hoboken, NJ: Wiley.

Paivio, Alan. 1986. *Mental Representations: A Dual Coding Approach.* Oxford: Oxford University Press.

——. 1991. *Images in Mind: The Evolution of a Theory.* New York: Harvester Wheatsheaf.

Paradi, David. 2015. "Results of the 2015 Annoying PowerPoint survey." http://www.thinkoutside-theslide.com/free-resources/latest-annoying-powerpoint-survey-results/.

Peterson, David. "Why Does the Rule of Thirds Work?" *Blog Post.* http://www.digital-photo-secrets.com/tip/2742/why-does-the-rule-of-thirds-work/.

Plass, Jan L., Steffi Heidig, Elizabeth O. Hayward, Bruce D. Homer, and Enjoon Um. 2014. "Emotional design in multimedia learning: Effects of shape and color on affect and learning." *Learning and Instruction* 29: 128–40.

Presentitude. 2014. "What Size Slide Should You Use?" November. http://presentitude.com/slide-size-use/.

Reynolds, Garr. 2008. "Slides (PDF) from Safari Webcast." http://www.slideshare.net/garr/slides-in-pdf-from-safari-webcast-presentation/12-How_to_thinklike_a_designerand.

Reynolds, Garr. 2010. *The Naked Presenter: Delivering Powerful Presentations With or Without Slides.* Berkeley, CA: New Riders.

——. 2011. *Presentation Zen: Simple Ideas on Presentation Design and Delivery,* 2nd edition. Berkeley, CA: New Riders.

——. 2013. *Presentation Zen Design: Simple Design Principles and Techniques to Enhance Your Presentations,* 2nd edition. Berkeley, CA: New Riders.

Rogowitz, Bernice E., and Lloyd A. Treinish. 1996. "What Should Engineers and Scientists Be Worried About Color?" *IBM Research Center.* http://www.research.ibm.com/people/l/lloydt/color/color.HTM.

Rouder, Jeffrey N., Richard D. Morey, Nelson Cowan, Christopher E. Zwilling, Candice C. Morey, and Michael S. Pratte. 2008. "An assessment of fixed-capacity models of visual working memory." *Proceedings of the National Academy of Sciences* 105 (16): 5975–79.

Skau, Drew and Robert Kosara. 2016. "Arcs, Angles, or Areas: Individual Data Encodings in Pie and Donut Charts." *Computer Graphics Forum (Proceedings EuroVis).* 35(3): 121–30.

Social Security Administration. 2009. "Fast Facts & Figures About Social Security, 2009." *Social Security Administration* (July). http://www.ssa.gov/policy/docs/chartbooks/fast_facts/2009/fast_facts09.pdf.

Social Security Administration. 2016. "Annual Statistical Supplement to the Social Security Bulletin, 2015." *Social Security Administration* (April). https://www.ssa.gov/policy/docs/statcomps /supplement/2015/.

Social Security Advisory Board. 2012. "Aspects of Disability Decision Making: Data and Materials." *Social Security Administration* (February). http://www.lb7.uscourts.gov/documents/1-11-CV-00224.pdf.

Song, Hyunjin, and Norbert Schwarz. "If It's Hard to Read, It's Hard to Do: Processing Fluency Affects Effort Prediction and Motivation." *Psychological Science* 19 (10): 986–8.

Spiekermann, Erik and E.M. Ginger. 2003. *Stop Stealing Sheep and Find Out How Type Works.* 2nd ed. Berkeley, CA: Adobe.

Stone, Maureen. 2006. "Choosing Colors for Data Visualization." BeyeNetwork Newsletter (January 17). http://www.b-eye-network.com/newsletters/ben/2235.

Stone, Maureen, 2013. *A Field Guide to Digital Color.* Boca Raton, FL: CRC Press.

Swinford, Echo, and Julie Terberg. 2012. *Building PowerPoint Templates Step by Step with the Experts.* Indianapolis, IN: Que.

Treisman, Anne. 1985. "Preattentive processing in vision" *Computer Vision, Graphics, and Image Processing* 31(2): 156–77.

Tufte, Edward. 2001. *The Visual Display of Quantitative Information,* 2nd edition. Cheshire, CT: Graphics Press.

U.S. Census Bureau. *Current Population Survey, 2011 to 2014 Annual Social and Economic Supplements.* http://www.census.gov/library/publications/2014/demo/p60-249.html

Williams, Robin. 2014. *The Non-Designer's Design Book,* 4th edition. Berkeley, CA: Peachpit.

Wong, Dona. 2010. *The Wall Street Journal Guide to Information Graphics: The Dos and Don'ts of Presenting Data, Facts, and Figures.* New York: Norton.

INDEX